Advance Praise for *Uncommon Service*

"If you believe in service excellence, you must read this book. In it you will discover the importance of making the right choices and trade-offs in your business model so that your team can consistently deliver uncommon service."

—Carlos Rodríguez-Pastor, Chairman, Interbank Group

"Frances Frei and Anne Morriss's *Uncommon Service* is a joy to read and a treasure to study. The authors provide both theories of how great service works and case studies that demonstrate how to make it happen. Always intuitive, never patronizing, and really smart, *Uncommon Service* will help any executive—in a big company or small, public firm or nonprofit organization—think creatively about how to deliver service that truly works."

—Debora Spar, President, Barnard College

"*Uncommon Service* is about how to deliver service excellence *by design*. It shows managers how to satisfy customers—not just on your organization's best days, but as an everyday routine."

—Tom Watson, Dean, Omnicom University; Cofounder and
Vice Chairman Emeritus, Omnicom Group, Inc.

UNCOMMON
SERVICE

*How to Win by Putting Customers
at the Core of Your Business*

UNCOMMON
SERVICE

FRANCES FREI | ANNE MORRISS

HARVARD BUSINESS REVIEW PRESS

Boston, Massachusetts

Library of Congress Cataloging-in-Publication Data

Frei, Frances.
    Uncommon service : how to win by putting customers at the core of your
business / Frances Frei, Anne Morriss.
      p. cm.
    ISBN 978-1-4221-3331-6 (alk. paper)
    1. Customer relations. 2. Customer services. 3. Service industries—
Management.   I. Morriss, Anne.   II. Title.
    HF5415.5.F728 2012
    658.8'12—dc23

                                                                2011029760

To our mothers and our sons,

who inspire us to serve

Contents

One of the gifts of working in academia is that you are surrounded by people who devote themselves to the art of education. They have no choice but to teach, and you have no choice but to learn, more often than not from every conversation. Throughout the book we have tried to celebrate the thinkers who have influenced us along the way, many of them colleagues who drive into the same parking lot every day. No doubt, we have fallen short.

We owe a particular debt of gratitude to the breakthrough work on services done by Ben Schneider and David Bowen, authors of *Winning on Service*, and Earl Sasser, Jim Heskett, and Len Schlesinger, authors of *The Service Profit Chain*. By capturing the importance of organizational design and the vital role that service employees play in building healthy companies, these books changed the way the world thought about the business of service. We have also been deeply influenced by the moral and intellectual courage of Clay Christensen, author of *The Innovator's Dilemma*. Clay has an extraordinary ability to distill out the essential truths of a complex world.

Our hope in writing this book is to give people the tools—and audacity—to go out and change organizations. Youngme Moon, author of *Different*, embodies this type of leadership. She has given us, and so many others, permission to dream.

Like Youngme, most of the messengers in this book study business. We don't typically associate service with the crass act of making money, yet for millions of people every day, the bulk of their human interactions takes place in a commercial setting. Do we really lose our humanity once we climb into the capitalist arena and add profit to the spoils? Of course not. Which means that we should be able to resolve the gap between the very human desire to serve and the frustrating service experiences we're now asking each other to endure. It is a gap, we believe, the world is ready to close.

If This Is a Service Economy, Why Am I Still on Hold?

We live and work in a service economy. In 1950, industrial workers represented the single largest employment sector in any developed country. Today, 80 percent of jobs are in service, and service represents 80 percent of the U.S. gross national product.

We cherish good service. In survey after survey, it's an enormous differentiator in our experience as consumers. Companies that deliver service excellence get a disproportionate share of our income, and our loyalty to them is often difficult to shake. In researching this book, we encountered more than a few people who were brought to tears as they recalled an empathetic insurance provider or an airline experience that made them feel human, despite their screaming infant or lost luggage.

We find deep meaning in the act of serving. We've been devising ways to take care of each other—and celebrating the results—since the human story was first documented. Developmental psychologists tell us that a willingness to help strangers is a trait that most people exhibit at as young an age as eighteen months. It's an almost universal impulse to serve, one that can get crowded out by other instincts, certainly, but if you peel back the layers of what motivates us, more often than not you'll find a very core ambition to be useful to others.

And yet. Good service is still, for the most part, rare. In our experience as economic actors, in industry across industry, we're increasingly frustrated and disappointed. Customers, employees, owners—no one wants to deliver bad service, and no one wants to endure it. But that's the experience we continue to inflict on each other.

Why is that?

This is the question that animates this book—why is service so hard to get right, despite the fact that we're wired for it? How can we channel the human impulse to serve into greater productivity, greater returns, and greater satisfaction all around?

Here's what we've learned: uncommon service is not born from attitude and effort, but from design choices made in the very blueprints of a business model. It's easy to throw service into a mission statement and periodically do whatever it takes to make a customer happy. What's hard is designing a service model that allows average employees—not just the exceptional ones—to produce service excellence as an everyday routine. Outstanding service organizations create offerings, funding strategies, systems, and cultures that set their people up to excel *casually*.

In this book, we try to show you how to do the same thing: how to deliver uncommon service by design. Building any dynamic system means considering inputs and outputs, actions and reactions, and many of the concepts here are rooted in basic engineering principles. But psychology is where we find some of the largest obstacles to excellence. These take the form of denying reality and resisting trade-offs, points that may seem counterintuitive—or at least counter-*comfortable.*

If you walked out on the street today and randomly asked someone to talk about a recent service experience, good or bad, chances are the person would recount a story of deep disappointment. We know this because we've personally developed a bad habit of invading strangers' personal space with questions like these. That story would probably involve a call center because, as we'll explain, call centers are designed to be reliably bad. But the story might just as easily be about wandering through department store aisles looking for a clerk to ring up an $8 pair of socks; or waiting for a shipment of parts that came in hopelessly late and hopelessly incomplete; or going through endless cycles with a voice-recognition unit ("For what you don't want, push or say 'four'"), trying every numerical option in the hope of getting through to some sympathetic soul who has an incentive to care that your son's talking Elmo won't say a word.

And yet we should be living through the Century of Service—so what's going on?

Be the Anti-Hero

Our message begins simply enough: you can't be good at everything. In services, trying to do it all brilliantly will lead almost inevitably to mediocrity. Excellence requires sacrifice. To deliver great service on the dimensions that your customers value most, you must underperform on dimensions they value less. This means you must have the stomach to do some things *badly.*

The concept can seem immoral at first blush. We recently did some work with a major health-care provider. The CEO wasn't able to join us until the last couple of days. When he arrived, we reviewed what we'd covered, including the link between underperformance and excellence. The CEO immediately pushed back, saying, "I don't see anything we could afford to be bad at." He continued, revealing that he saw the idea of lowering the bar on any dimension as dishonorable, particularly in a field like health care. Hands immediately shot up around the room. His team disagreed, and after listening to their ideas for where trade-offs could be made—where resources could be shifted from areas low on the customers' priority list to areas customers cared more about—the CEO finally backed down. "I get it," he said. "That's how we can afford to be great."

Charismatic leaders sometimes assume that they can avoid this trade-off by sheer force of personality. If they just get everybody fired up, the kinks will work themselves out. But you can't design a system that is based on the faith that all of your employees will perform heroically, all day, every day, for an indefinite period. For a system to work, excellence must be normalized. And you don't get to that point by demanding extraordinary sacrifice. You get there by designing a model where the full spectrum of your employees—not just the outstanding ones—will have no choice but to deliver excellence as an everyday routine. You get there by building a system that just doesn't produce anything else.

Heroism, in fact, can be a red flag. We know a service recovery expert who comes in early and stays late every day, picking up the slack and overcoming the obstacles in her company's service design. Whenever a client has had enough and is about to walk, she gets on the case and, through her superhuman effort, "fixes" everything. But as long as she's around, the company will never confront the serious problems they've created for themselves, the money they're leaving on the table, and the growth opportunities they're missing—to say nothing of the risk of assuming that this very special employee will stick around. Cynicism can build quickly among talented, client-facing people when service problems are systematically tolerated. The cape starts to feel heavy when it's overused.

Great service, it turns out, is not made possible by running the business harder and faster on the backs of a few extraordinary people. It's made possible—profitable, sustainable, scalable—by designing a system that sets up everyone to excel.

The Four Service Truths

Once you accept the idea of trade-offs—and break the addiction to service heroes—the inputs into service excellence are much easier to consume. We lay out these inputs in a framework we call the *four service truths,* which are the assumptions behind the basic elements of a successful, high-service model: a service offering, a service funding mechanism, an employee management system, and a customer management system (figure I-1). These four truths act as the mental cornerstones of a sustainable model for delivering uncommon service:

FIGURE I-1

Principles of service excellence: leverage trade-offs, funding, employees, and customers

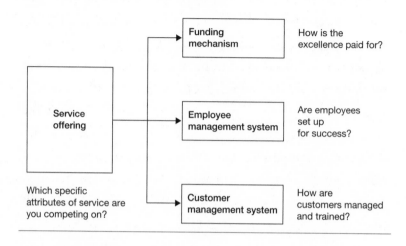

1. *You can't be good at everything.* You must be bad in the service of good. Excellence requires under-performing on the dimensions your customers value least so that you can overperform on the dimensions your customers value most. Once you choose this path, the decision on where to be good and bad should by driven by deep insight into who your customers are and what they need *operationally.*

2. *Someone has to pay for it.* Service excellence must be funded in some way. You can find a palatable way to charge your customers more for it, reduce costs while improving your service experience, or get customers to do some of the work for you. Choosing among these strategies—finding the right funding mechanism for your business—will depend on both industry

dynamics (e.g., price sensitivity) and the specific relationship you have with your customers.

3. *It's not your employees' fault.* Your people matter, but not because they're the make-or-break input on delivering uncommon service. What matters more is the way you've designed your service model, in particular, the way the model sets up average people to excel as a matter of routine. Rather than creating an environment where employees have the time and space to focus on satisfying customers, many service organizations today are actually undermining their people's ability to serve.

4. *You must manage your customers.* You must be deliberate about involving your customers in creating—not just consuming—your service experience. In other words, you also need a management plan for your customers. To return to our manufacturing metaphor, the special challenge of service delivery is that your customers routinely wander onto the shop floor—unannounced—and tinker with the assembly line. And yet success isn't just a matter of keeping them out of trouble. Your customers need to play a productive role on the line itself, and to do so, they need training, guidance, safety goggles—and more.

Finally, you need to unleash that service model in an organizational culture that reinforces it at every turn. Getting the service design right is only half the challenge. The other half is creating a culture that's sufficiently aligned with that model. In services, in particular, culture defines an enormous part of the stakeholder experience—every employee decision, every customer touch point. With clients wandering the shop floor, there's no keeping the ugly truth contained in the back office.

In our work, we often ask people to wrestle with this definition of leadership. Leadership, at its core, is about making other people better as a result of your presence—*and making sure that the impact lasts in your absence.* As a leader, you create the conditions for others (in services, that means employees *and* customers to perform), and you do what it takes to sustain those conditions, even when you're not in the room. Designing good systems is part of this "absentee leadership," but the most powerful tool you have, by far, is culture. Culture not only guides individual decision-making, but also provides the foundation for all other organizational behavior and action. In other words, culture doesn't just tell you what to do—it shows you how to think.

We see it this way:

$$\text{Service Excellence} = \text{Design} \times \text{Culture}$$

Each factor in our service-excellence equation is weighted equally, which allows for some wiggle room. A stronger culture can partly make up for a weaker design, and vice versa. But if either one is neglected, you're stuck. Excellence is definitively beyond your reach.

If your ambition is to grow, our advice is to first get your own equation in order. Get a high level of control over your service design and culture, understand the levers that drive each one, and then use them more strategically. We do our best in the following pages to guide you on that journey. Once you're in control, you basically have two choices when it comes to getting bigger: do more of what you're already doing, or do different things. In our worldview, doing more of what you're already doing means growing the existing service model. Doing different things means building new service models. Both paths are viable, but there are specific challenges to each.

Cast of Characters

We break up these concepts for the sake of pedagogy, but in fact our message is highly integrative. It doesn't work to just focus on a subset of these concepts; you have to go after them as a whole. And so we revisit many of the same companies throughout the book to illustrate how the parts work together. Of course, we supplement these stories with many others along the way, but here's an introduction to some of the protagonists that will be making multiple cameos (in order of appearance):

> *Commerce Bank*—With an unconventional business model that broke the unspoken rules of customer engagement, Commerce Bank became the fastest growing retail bank in America.

> *Southwest Airlines*—A favorite of business school professors, Southwest remains an exception to the rule that airlines must lose money and make their customers miserable. And it has done so by proving that uncommon service isn't the exclusive domain of high-priced, high-end offerings.

Ochsner Health System—Ochsner is delivering world-class patient care in communities still recovering from the aftermath of Hurricane Katrina, while taking a leadership role in transforming the U.S. health-care industry. Despite the cost sensitivity of its patient population and the operational complexity of health care, Ochsner is refusing to produce anything less than excellence.

Bugs Burger Bug Killers—In an industry where competitors only promised to do their best, BBBK became a sensation by *guaranteeing* complete customer satisfaction. But it meant that business as usual wasn't possible. Everyone, particularly clients, had to work a lot harder.

Magazine Luiza—This huge Brazilian retailer provides exceptional service to an unconventional market: poor, "unbanked" rural customers who are often not functionally literate. For the model to work, the company had to develop creative, new systems for managing customers and meeting their needs.

LSQ Funding Group—LSQ uses an innovative service design not only to revolutionize the value it creates for small businesses, but also to set its employees up to excel as a matter of routine. By embedding much of the job's operations in an intuitive information technology (IT) system, LSQ enables its employees to deliver uncommon service literally on day one.

Zappos—The high-profile Internet retailer has designed a winning service model, which it gladly shares with the growing number of observers who want to study it.

That's because the real driver of its extraordinary success is much harder to copy: an organizational culture that brazenly challenges the most basic assumptions about what work and commerce are supposed to feel like.

We want to stress here that we're looking at these and other organizations at a moment in time, when the choices they made had something special to teach the world. It doesn't mean that these companies retained their status as role models. Like many companies, some of them lost their momentum, if not their ways entirely. Sometimes this happens because of integration realities—a company's service model and culture simply get absorbed or diluted by its buyer.[1] And sometimes a company is bought by new owners who don't fully understand the origins of their acquisition's exceptional success. They skillfully run the numbers, but they don't see the links between finance and operations clearly enough. We hope to expose those links, for both current managers of service companies and those who may replace them in the future.

The Commitment to Serve

In short, we want to be helpful. Our collaboration was born from the shared belief that the commitment to serve is ingrained in the human soul—and the shared observation that this commitment often fails to translate into sustained acts of service, even with the best of intentions. Frances first saw this challenge in her academic research and while in the trenches with executives trying to improve service in their own companies. Anne first saw it on the front lines of mission-driven organizations in the public and nonprofit sectors. Good people with good ideas were not enough.

Our ambition, with this book, is to help you build an organization that truly reflects your humanity, one that can shamelessly deliver uncommon service.

Chapter One

Truth Number 1:
You Can't Be Good
at Everything

Vernon Hill is a banker who started out in real estate, scouting new locations for retailers. One of his first clients was McDonald's, and some say the Happy Meal inspired him. One thing is clear: as the founder and CEO of Commerce Bank, he built a wildly successful enterprise that rewrote the rules of an industry. And he did it by daring to be bad.

We feature the story of Vernon Hill's creation—Commerce Bank—because it allows us to show how a company can design a great service offering, largely by making a series of carefully chosen and carefully integrated trade-offs.

When Hill started out in 1973, his vision was to build a bank not in the image of the leading financial institutions but modeled after the most successful retailers. Conventional wisdom at the time was that banks grew by offering the most attractive interest rates on deposits. The industry also assumed that the best way to accelerate growth was to aggressively acquire other banks. Commerce offered the worst rates in the industry, made very few acquisitions, and yet became the fastest growing retail bank in America. Its dynamism drove a 2,000 percent rise in its stock price in the 1990s.

The bank achieved its success by deciding to be great at some dimensions of service and bad at others. Not casually bad, but bad in the service of great.

A Strategy in Plain View

Commerce Bank carved out a winning position by deciding very strategically where it would excel—and by understanding very clearly what that would mean for the rest of its service model. Hill started by dwelling on the obvious: customers hated his competitors' limited hours and bad attitudes. *Bankers hours* had been a term of derision for decades. For people with jobs, kids, or a commute, or all of these, the fact that a bank teller's window might be open from ten to four, five days a week, was almost offensive. And then there was the less-than-welcoming behavior of the tellers behind those windows and the loan officers sitting stoically nearby. The sullen or imperious bank employee had been a stock character in comedy going all the way back to vaudeville.

These cultural clichés meant that Commerce's potential lines of attack—inconvenience, lack of customer appreciation—were just as open to the established banks as they were to Hill. So how did Commerce claim competitive advantage in the area of hours and attitude? The company created a service model based on a series of integrated trade-offs that its competitors were unwilling (and perhaps unable) to make.

With a target set of customers—those who were fed up with the service experience of a traditional retail bank—clearly in mind, Commerce set out to design a model of excellence. Aiming to be best on hours, the bank chose to stay open seven days a week. Monday through Friday, you could bank at Commerce from 7:30 a.m. to 8:00 p.m. On Friday evenings, drive-through windows would be open until midnight, and full-service banking would be available Saturdays and Sundays. This would give Commerce the most convenient hours in the business, earning its tagline of America's Most Convenient Bank. But this kind of convenience was an expensive proposition. Indeed, the expense of being open for extended hours was a primary reason that the competition avoided it.

Why could Commerce pull it off? Because of its product design choices. Commerce paid the lowest rates on deposits in every local market. The additional capital this choice generated gave the company the resources to fund better hours. In other words, convenient hours and lower rates were inextricably linked. Commerce could deliver excellence in hours precisely because of its dismal deposit rates.

We've seen this pattern across excellent service organizations, regardless of industry, geography, or positioning. Like Commerce, these organizations do a lot of things well, but they also—counterintuitively—do certain things badly. Really badly. Their trick is to make sure that the bad is in service of the great, and then to be unapologetic about it.

This point is crucial to understanding how to design uncommon service. In our experience, the number one obstacle to great service—number one by a long shot—is the emotional unwillingness to embrace weakness. But it couldn't be clearer that to win in one area, you must lose in another. Progress requires sacrifice. Some part of your service offering must be thrown under the bus.

Nevertheless, choosing bad can feel like an assault on the soul. Choosing bad means deliberately letting people down, giving up a can-do, anything's-possible attitude toward adversity. Choosing bad feels bad, particularly in mission-driven industries such as health care or education, where managers feel a moral imperative to at least *try* in all areas. That's not, of course, how we see it. Choosing bad is your only shot at achieving greatness. And resisting it is a recipe for mediocrity.

Tough Choices

How do you decide where to be good and where to be bad? Commerce Bank knew that its target customers cared much more about longer hours than about competitive rates on deposits. And so competitive rates were the first thing on the chopping block. But the company didn't settle for being just average or slightly below average. Commerce chose to be terrible, with literally the worst rates in every local market. Our version of its informal tagline is "No one will pay you less for your money."

This was the first of a few critical trade-offs. Commerce Bank also wanted to be best in class in customer interactions. It wanted to build an outstanding customer experience driven by the cheerful service orientation of its frontline people. And so it started by investigating the employee dynamics in its industry. What the company found—and what we have seen across industries—is that hiring employees who are the

FIGURE 1-1

Employees who rate high on multiple measures are expensive to hire

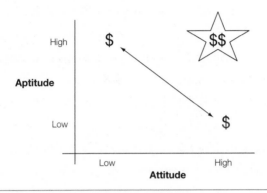

best-of-the-best in both attitude and aptitude is an expensive proposition. Everyone loves happy competence, and it's a seller's market for this kind of talent, even in rocky economic times. As a result, these employees can cost up to twice as much as employees who excel on only one of these two dimensions (figure 1–1). The rate for these cream-of-the-crop employees was prohibitively expensive for the retail banking industry.

Commerce Bank could in no way afford the expense of hiring the best in both attitude and aptitude. So it chose one: attitude. The bank set out to deliver the best attitude in all of banking, focusing its hiring almost exclusively on enthusiasm and interpersonal skills. These friendly recruits quickly blew the doors off the industry's reputation for surly service. Commerce Bank employees were nice! Happy! Empathetic! With open hearts, they greeted customers at the door with newspapers and walked them to their cars in bad weather. They signed up for the itinerant corporate Wow Patrol, traveling from branch to branch to make sure that colleagues and customers were having a great time. In these ways and more, Commerce made the sober business of banking fun.

But by not investing in aptitude, Commerce could have put itself at risk. People with limited technical skills, no matter how pleasant, could not eloquently parse the distinctions between twenty-seven varieties of checking accounts, much less rapidly explain complex financial instruments to wary investors. So to accommodate this design choice, Commerce Bank simplified its product set. Dramatically. Commerce basically sold you a checking account, period, which made the bank dead last in the industry's celebrated cross-sell metric.

But the decision also delivered a first-place showing on pleasant branch experiences. To gain the freedom to hire the employees it needed, the bank chose not to be merely below average in product range and innovation, but categorically the worst. And in return, Commerce customers got what *they* wanted—the friendliest interactions in all of banking.

Notice what Commerce has done. It's worst in class on some service dimensions (rates and product mix) so that it can be best in class on others (hours and attitude). Bad in the service of great. It sounds simple, but the courage to choose low deposit rates and poor cross-sell performance seemed crazy alongside the desire to grow. These choices worked because being bad was not a missed opportunity, but rather was the fuel to create an exceptional service experience.

Figure 1–2 captures Commerce's relative performance on the service dimensions we've just discussed. For the vertical axis, it's as if we were able to read the mind of Commerce customers and learn which service feature is most important

FIGURE 1-2

Commerce Bank's relative performance on service dimensions

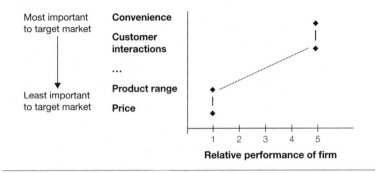

to them, which feature is next most important, and so on. Notice that Commerce is indeed a collection of 5's (best) and 1's (worst). The bank was so successful because it had the wisdom to know the difference, to know where it should be winning and losing. Being worst in class on the things that were least important to its customers allowed it to be best in class at the things that were most important to them. That's the trick. You have to be bad in the service of great—and you have to be very smart about which is which.

We can follow the same logic for other successful service organizations. Let's start with some well-known examples. Consider Southwest Airlines. On the strategy graph in figure 1–3—a great visualization tool developed by a Harvard Business School colleague, Jan Rivkin—the attributes ranging from most important to least important for Southwest's target customers have been arranged on the vertical axis. For clarity, we will call these strategy graphs *attribute maps*. On Southwest's attribute map, you can see that low prices top the

FIGURE 1-3

Attribute map for Southwest Airlines (SWA)

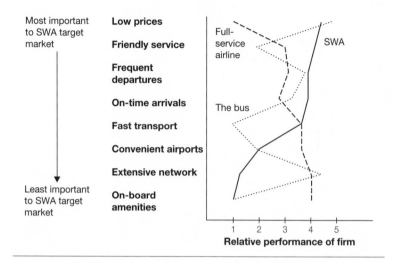

list, with friendly service in the number two spot. At the bottom, the items of least importance are an extensive network and on-board amenities. But also note Southwest's performance. It's best in class on the attributes that matter the most to its customers and worst in class on those that matter the least.

The same holds true for Walmart. The attributes that range from most important to least important for Walmart's target customers have been arranged on the vertical axis of an attribute map (figure 1–4). The low-prices attribute tops the list, with selection across categories in the number two spot. At the bottom, the items of least importance are sales help and ambiance.

Walmart's performance over the past thirty years suggests that the retailer knows its customers very well and that it is indeed meeting its customers' needs. But notice that the company—just like Commerce Bank and Southwest—is not excellent or even average at everything. Indeed, its service offering is a collection of above-average and below-average attributes, moving to either extreme at the top and bottom of the list.[1]

Walmart executives aren't likely to be shocked to learn that their stores are harshly lit environments with sporadic sales support. These choices reduce the cost of operations, which gives the stores the flexibility to charge customers less for a wide range of products. These choices funded the company's excellence in other, more important dimensions. Walmart had the stomach to let its customers solve their own problems in an uninspired setting in exchange for "always low prices," a deal their customers were happy to make.

FIGURE 1-4

Attribute map for Walmart

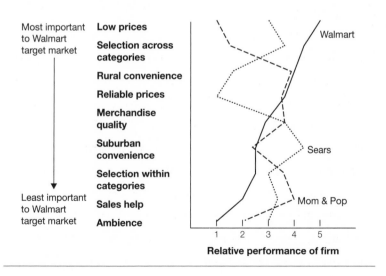

How do you strike this kind of deal with your own customers? Commerce Bank started by going after customer pain points that were widely known and well understood, both among customers and by senior managers. We've seen these kinds of well-understood customer pain points in almost every industry. It's no secret that the cable service technician who may turn up at nine in the morning—or then again maybe not until four in the afternoon—makes everyone crazy. Similarly, everyone knows that customers hate being locked into a long service contract with a cell phone provider. It's not that companies aren't aware of these pain points. It's that they're convinced they can't afford to address them.

Most executives think they can't afford the cost of service improvement. It's too complex (and thus expensive) to schedule home service calls with precision. And cell phone providers *have no choice* but to chain a customer to their service contract in order to subsidize the handset purchase. These perceptions become reality—until a competitor like Commerce exposes them as ridiculous.[2]

Let's pause here and answer some questions we sometimes hear when we talk about this concept. Haven't we heard parts of this message before? Isn't good strategy about knowing what you won't do? Yes, it is. And as a parallel, you can think of service excellence as knowing what you won't do *well.* In our experience, this decision can be a lot harder. Walmart's leadership didn't decide not to have stores with ambiance. Instead, the company decided to let the ambiance of its stores be worse than that of their competitors, just as Hill and his team decided that Commerce would offer the worst rates and the most limited product set in the entire industry. It's often harder to do something badly than to not do it at all, particularly when it means disappointing your customers. The choice to let stakeholders down cuts to the core of a manager's identity. In some cases, it can feel like a challenge to your integrity, as if you're choosing to under-deliver on your commitment to your fellow human beings.

On the other side, of course, may be your one chance to fulfill it.

Enter Kiva

Kiva—which describes itself as "the world's first online lending platform"—connects individual lenders to poor entrepreneurs around the world. The total value of Kiva's loan portfolio hit the remarkable $200 million milestone early in 2011, at an average loan size of less than $400.

Kiva's vision is nothing less than to create a world where everyone, even in the most impoverished, war-torn corners of the globe, has the ability to create opportunity. But this world would remain solidly out of reach unless the organization made some critical trade-offs in its service model.

Here's where Kiva decided to excel: most organizations in the global development business collect money from a network of "customers" (also known as donors), keep some percentage to fund their operations, then spend the rest as they see fit, typically to support clients in faraway places. Donors typically have no idea who these clients are and have little say in how or where their donations are spent. But Kiva made the radical choice to remove the organization-as-intermediary and link donors directly to clients.[a] Kiva lets donors decide for themselves which clients to lend to and exactly how much to lend. For the segment of donors that Kiva is targeting, that kind of transparency and control tops the donors' list of their service priorities. As a result, Kiva's donors—572,000 and counting—are disproportionately, passionately satisfied. The month-to-month growth rate of its loan portfolio averages 30 percent.

What makes the experience so different? As a Kiva donor, you can, for example, go to the Web site, scroll through the various loan requests, and decide to help someone named Busena buy a motorbike to expand her charcoal business in rural Sudan. She needs $100 more to purchase the bike, and you decide to make up the difference. You have your own reasons for betting on Busena. You may think her success will have a meaningful impact on women and girls in rural Sudan, a population that is among the poorest and most disenfranchised in the world, and you may believe deeply in the transformative power of role models for marginalized groups. Those could be your investment criteria.

Kiva is not asking you to trust someone else's criteria in a large, opaque bureaucracy. And it's letting Busena decide how to lift herself out of poverty. A model that does

FIGURE 1-5

Attribute map for Kiva

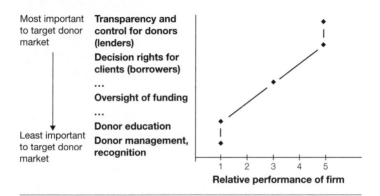

Most important to target donor market

Transparency and control for donors (lenders)

Decision rights for clients (borrowers)

...

Oversight of funding

...

Donor education

Least important to target donor market

Donor management, recognition

Relative performance of firm

not strip Busena of her decision rights is another priority for Kiva's target donors. Kiva donors tend to believe that traditional, charity-focused aid is a far less effective way to fight poverty.

What's the trade-off? To fund the development of a robust IT infrastructure, Kiva has to forgo investing heavily in other kinds of donor services, such as educating donors on global issues or thanking donors for their support at a prestigious annual dinner. And its reduced overhead means that it has to rely on volunteer labor for key organizational functions such as monitoring and evaluating loan performance (figure 1–5). But it turns out Kiva donors are more than willing to make those trade-offs—and no one feels bad about it. In exchange, they get to help create opportunity in places the world has forgotten, for as little as $25.

Kiva, too, found a way to be bad in the service of great.

a. Kiva prefers the terms *lender* and *borrower* to describe its key stakeholders, as these terms are better at capturing the dignity of the relationship. For clarity of the example, we've chosen to stick with *donor* and *client.*

The Cipriani Exception

When we discuss the need to be "bad" with executives, we often see flashes of understanding and agreement, but we also meet resistance. We regularly confront a team's conviction that this rule may apply to other companies, but surely not to theirs. We see it in the audience's shifting posture, people's unwillingness to make direct eye contact. Eventually we're peppered with a volley of defiant statements—"But we're [insert company name here]! We have to be good at everything!" We typically just ask, "And how's that working out for you?" And rarely do we hear an answer that doesn't feature exhausted employees, frustrated customers, and disappointed investors. Our point is simply that this dissatisfaction is a predictable outcome—when you're trying to be great at everything.

To help executives wrestle with this idea, we offer the example of Orient Express Hotels, Ltd. (OEH), which includes in its network of world-class, high-end hotels the incredible Hotel Cipriani in Venice. OEH establishments are designed to be a 5 out of 5 on every service dimension. At the Cipriani, you can rent a palazzo with your own private butler, as well as adjacent dock space for your yacht. But even if you travel by the more pedestrian airplane, you can still relish the Rubelli fabrics draping windows and chairs, as you dine on orecchiette cooked by master chef Renato Piccolotto, who has been exploring Venetian cuisine since 1970. Everything at the Cipriani is exquisite and made to order according to local traditions that date back centuries. But here's the catch: OEH hotels such as the Cipriani charge a 50 percent price premium over the number two competitor in their local markets. And the number two competitor might be the Four Seasons. If your market will give you a 50 percent price premium on the service you're offering, then you, too, can deliver perfection across the board. In this economic moment, however, we found very few companies that live in that world.

In other words, the vast majority of organizations have two options (figure 1–6). Option B (trying to excel in all attributes, but settling for less across the board) is emotionally easier and quite a bit less risky for individuals. With this option,

FIGURE 1-6

Options for companies deciding whether—and where—to be "bad"

Y-axis: Key service attributes (in order of priority to target market)
X-axis: Relative performance of firm

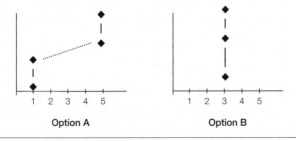

you don't really need to understand your customers. Even if their preferences evolve—even if the ordering of attributes on the vertical axis changes—you're still fine. In contrast, option A (excelling in some attributes and doing poorly in others) can be terrifying. You have to choose where to focus on excellence, and there are real costs to getting it wrong. Option A makes option B start to look more appealing—until you're reminded that option B leaves you stuck in mediocrity.

Beyond risk aversion, there's another psychological pull toward option B. It's simply human nature to want to avoid weakness or to use your weaknesses as a guide for where to improve. Indeed, most gap analyses are built on this idea and then color-coded to reinforce the point: hunt down your biggest flaws (the red ones), and improve them; now move quickly on to the yellow ones. But this approach can be a disaster. When your weaknesses are enabling your strengths, reducing the gaps between you and your competitors can actually undermine performance, turning a well-intentioned improvement effort into a strategically dangerous paint-by-number exercise.

The Laws of Physics Still Apply

As provocative as the notion of being bad in the service of great is for service managers, it's almost boring for product managers. Those who manufacture for a living are perplexed at why those who don't are resistant to the idea of being-bad-to-be-good. To help explain why, consider the MacBook Air. When Apple set out to be best in class on the lightness of its newest laptop, the company understood that the product may have to be worst in class on memory. Of course, every year,

Apple's engineers try to push the frontier and improve on both dimensions, but at any one moment, everyone understands that these features trade off on each other.

Apple isn't generally filled with angst over the trade-off. The company knows that if it puts in too much memory (or a host of other features), it risks destroying the laptop's dramatic weight advantage. Like most producers of physical products, Apple managers are used to confronting the laws of physics. Volvo's engineers know that they have to choose safety over sporty. Designers of Zara's trendy, low-priced clothing make their model work by using low-cost materials over durable ones. These decision makers get to touch and feel the trade-offs. They know that they can't have it all. And by no means does it reduce their pride in their work. Quite the opposite, these companies understand that by honoring constraints, they get the privilege of delivering excellence.

People working within the limits of the physical product space tend to have an easier time with the concept of trade-offs. For example, a widespread rule in the construction business states that a customer can expect two of the following three things: speed, quality, and price. You can get good quality built quickly, but it will cost you. You can get something built fast and cheap, but the quality will suffer. Or you can get good quality for a competitive price, but the wait will be painful. This is also known as the *impossible triangle*. It's considered irrational to ask for all three.

Our goal is to bring this same kind of intuition to service managers. Service managers often behave as if the laws of physics don't apply to them. Without blushing, they make it their goal to be the lowest-cost, highest-quality, fastest-moving service providers. Many managers also believe that they're inspiring the troops by demanding it all. In our experience, the opposite often occurs. Cynicism can build quickly among frontline employees who are confronting the trade-offs every day, while their managers continue to deny reality.

Putting It into Practice

In our work, we recommend a diagnostic phase where you create your own attribute maps, similar to the ones we showed you for Commerce Bank, Southwest Airlines, Walmart, and Kiva. This process will help surface not only what is most and least important to your customers, but also how well your performance is aligned with those preferences.

The basic idea is straightforward. On the vertical axis, list the distinct elements of the service offering, in order of importance *according to your customers*. In other words, list in descending order the service attributes that your target customer considers most important. On the horizontal axis, chart how well you're doing, again from the perspective of the customer. Then add to this how well the competition is doing along the same dimensions.

The exercise is often easier said than done. What follows is guidance that should be useful as you set out to do this for your own organization. We're going to recommend that you do the exercise twice; once internally without input from customers or competitors, and then with external data. Why bother with the first pass? The process forces you to develop and clarify your research hypotheses, but it can also bring to light any hidden inconsistencies in how employees are thinking about customers and competitors. Exposing these inconsistencies can serve as powerful motivation to get everyone on the same page.

We often refer to this first internal step as the sanding that's necessary before applying a layer of paint, a favorite teaching metaphor. Learning occurs when people are open to it. Changing hearts and minds sometimes requires unlocking them first. This is particularly true in organizations that have been in business for a while or in cultures where improvement isn't celebrated at all levels of the firm. When your organization creates an internal attribute map, you often discover that people are working with radically different assumptions about customers and competitors, which can be productively terrifying—and highly motivating to get closer to the truth.

Step 1: Create an Internal Attribute Map

To create an internal attribute map for your organization, you need to put together groups of a workable size—big enough to include diverse thinking but small enough to discourage passive participation from anyone. We like groups of five to seven people. In our experience, *diagonal representation* works best for these kinds of activities. You want a mix of perspectives on the team, so we recommend representatives from across business units, as well as representatives from different levels in the hierarchy. Mix it up with operations and sales units, frontline and back-office people, those with lots of decision rights and those no decision rights at all. With the group assembled, task them with creating a service attribute map for one of the organization's most important markets.

Ask the group to channel the market's most important customers. If you had a few customers in front of you and had windows into their souls, what would they be thinking and feeling? What would they value? Brainstorm all of the elements of the service experience that are relevant to these customers.

The output of this is what we call a *cloud* of attributes. The next step is to order these attributes from the most important to the least important *from the perspective of the customer.* Write down which attribute you think your customers care most about, and then the next, and the next. It is at this stage that different views of the customer's perspective typically surface. Dwell on this tension. Really honor it. As employees try to persuade each other that they're right, it reveals important divergence in an organization's attitudes about its customers, how strongly held those beliefs are, and whether there's sufficient empirical evidence to support these beliefs. (Note: there rarely is.)

If a consensus can't be reached, we recommend moving forward with a simple democratic process. Ask people to vote for their top three customer priorities with a checkmark. The attribute with the most checkmarks is candidate for being first, and so on.

Marketing Versus Operating Segments, or, What If My Customers Want Different Things?

The attribute discussion often reveals that different customers within a target segment are likely to value things differently. This is very important to identify. While most organizations can describe the profiles of their target markets relatively easily (soccer moms!), organizations often struggle to articulate with sufficient operational detail the distinctions in their customers' needs. The ability to do so is crucial to designing and delivering service excellence.

We have come to describe the way most companies segment their customers as *marketing segments*—the buckets used to identify and communicate with different kinds of customers. We call the classifying of customers by service priorities *operating segments*. The vertical axis created in an attribute map can be thought of as an operating segment. The goal of the diagnostic stage is to reveal all the different operating segments—that is, all the different orderings of attributes that you are currently serving.

Operating segments and marketing segments sometimes line up perfectly, but many managers discover that they're trying to serve more than one operating segment within a single marketing segment. Consider a preschool we studied. The school had clearly identified the types of families that fit best with its culture and philosophy regarding early childhood education. And so the school was working hard to recruit young families who believed in a focus on cultivating connection and curiosity rather than formal knowledge-building—numbers and letters—in toddlers. The school was also looking for families who were interested in outsourcing curricular decision rights to the professionals (versus a high-involvement, co-op model). All of its targeting decisions were driven by this psychographic profiling.

Within this marketing segment, however, the school discovered two operating segments with very distinct service needs: (1) families with parents in the formal workforce and

(2) families with a parent at home during the day. It turned out there were stark differences in the service preferences of these two segments, which had major implications for the operations of the school. Working parents prioritized a school day that lasted from at least 8:30 to 5:30, regular remote communications with teachers, and after-hours services such as parent education. Stay-at-home parents, in contrast, valued face-to-face communications with teachers during afternoon pickup, the chance to volunteer for school events, and meetings that did not interrupt the dinner hour. Each segment shared the same educational goals and values—and each segment defined service excellence very differently.

The school's administration eventually reached a decision point that many organizations confront: should the school optimize for one operating segment or build a model that could serve multiple segments? We'll explore that question in detail shortly. At this point, the focus is on identifying the operating segments. How many are there? For each one, create a separate attribute map.

After your customers' priorities have been entered on the vertical axis, it's time to rank yourself and your competitors along each dimension. This again requires channeling your most important customers. Revisit that window into their souls. How do you and your competitors size up on each dimension? Use a basic scale of 1 to 5, and rank yourselves and your primary competitors.

This is another step where you're likely to draw out different perspectives within your own internal team. Again, embrace this tension. Bring it out into the light, where it can live and breathe and teach you things. At this step, too, we often hear that customers don't have complete information, that an organization's superior performance is a well-kept industry secret. This may be the case. For now, take your customers' perspective. Rank yourself according to what your customers currently think about you and your competitors.

With the above information, you should now be in a position to take a first pass at your attribute maps, one for each operating segment. When we go over the results with client companies, we often get a strong reaction. Sometimes, it is stunned silence; sometimes, gasps of recognition. Often, we've divided executives from a single company into five or more teams and told them all to do this exercise on the same target market. As often as not, we get five or more charts. This alone is important data. It means an organization is unproductively diffused, sometimes living in entirely different realities—and unlikely to be optimized for what its customers truly value.

Wait: What Exactly Is an Attribute?

The creation of an internal attribute map can sometimes lead to some philosophical and semantic tangles. For instance, when do you double-click on a single preference and open it up into several attributes, and when can you condense several preferences into one?

Let's say you come up with service or convenience as attributes that your customer values. But *convenience* could embody several elements. It could mean "location nearby," or it could mean "open twenty-four hours." How do you choose? The test is this: if you broke apart what might appear to be a single attribute and ranked the individual subelements, would those pieces then appear sequentially on the list, or separately?

And if all of those subelements appeared independently, would you and your competitors score consistently across them?

If the different subelements show up widely separated in the rankings, then they cannot be collapsed into a single attribute. If they rank sequentially—and your performance compared with your peers is equivalent and stable—then it makes sense to consider them a single attribute.

Step 2: Create an External Attribute Map

Now it's time to bring in your customers. Unfortunately, simply asking customers to rank their priorities from 1 to 15 rarely works. Real people don't think or talk this way. Instead, we recommend designing an interaction that encourages customers to *reveal* their preferences. The truth lies somewhere between the customer's act of revealing and the manager's act of inferring.

An extreme-sports version of this process, *conjoint analysis,* can take a long time and cost a lot of money. You take a bunch of attributes, break them into pairs, and then ask customers which they prefer. It's a technique for getting people to reveal their preferences without asking them directly. A classic example is from the auto industry: Would you prefer satellite radio or four-wheel drive? Then, depending on the answer, you ask another pairwise comparison, then another. At the end of the process, customers reliably reveal their preferences, even when it would have been difficult for those same customers to clearly state them up front.

Aside from the time and expense of traditional conjoint analysis, a problem with this approach is that the output is only as good as the questions. You may go to all this trouble and not know if the attributes you're testing are even the right ones. In contrast, we recommend talking with customers and getting them to talk to you about the service offering. Give yourself the freedom to customize for each person, and proceed in a more sensitive and qualitative way. This way, you can learn about attributes that may not have occurred to you, and you can tell if someone is put off or confused by your questions. You can pivot by asking new questions or asking existing questions in another way.

We advise doing this kind of modified conjoint analysis or qualitative conjoint analysis—at least as a first step. Talk to a random selection of customers. You choose them randomly because a convergence of opinion in a random selection will give you more confidence than a convergence (or divergence) of opinion otherwise. You'll be sure that you're reading meaningful signals. And the randomness will permit you to learn more quickly.

CASE STUDY

Ochsner Health System

We know this process works, because we've spent a lot of time understanding companies with these tools. One such company is Ochsner Health System, the largest nonprofit integrated health-care system in Louisiana. We were invited by the company president and chief operating officer, Warner Thomas, to help the organization achieve its goal of world-class patient care in New Orleans and surrounding areas, a region still recovering from the aftermath of Hurricane Katrina. Thomas and his team were passionate about delivering excellence in communities that felt forgotten or underserved by a range of institutions. Their goal was to create a model that treated its patients, employees, and owners with dignity.

For Ochsner, we did a few dozen customer interviews, each ranging from thirty minutes to an hour. One of the central questions we pursued was, "Under what circumstances do you use Ochsner for your health care versus other competitors?" What you're looking for with a question like this is insight into the changing circumstances that send your customers either to you or to your competitors. The answer often reveals what really matters to a customer, and that's what you want to listen for.

Is it location that motivates a customer, or costs? Or is it something else entirely that you didn't think of? Are these preferences locked in, or do they depend on the circumstances? In health care, we often hear patients say things like this: "For routine procedures, I don't want to give up my whole day. But for more complicated things, I'm willing to travel to get to a hospital and sit in a waiting room, waiting for the best doctor." An individual patient often has several hierarchies of attributes, in fact, depending on his or her particular health-care needs.

For Ochsner, we discovered that there were four distinct hierarchies of attributes, or operating segments. The segments were distinguished by the complexity of the services (high risk or low risk) and by the urgency of the care needed (planned or unplanned). We had no idea that this breakdown was going to emerge when we began the

FIGURE 1-7

39 · You Can't Be Good at Everything

Operating segments for customers of Ochsner Health System

	Planned	Unplanned
High risk	**Back surgery** • Quality of care • Coordination of care • Convenience/location • Time to appointment • Waiting time	**Breast cancer treatment** • Time to appointment • Quality of care • Coordination of care • Waiting time • Convenience/location
Low risk	**Yearly physical** • Convenience/location • Waiting time • Quality of care • Coordination of care • Time to appointment	**Flu** • Convenience/location • Time to appointment • Waiting time • Quality of care • Coordination of care

process, and we discovered these categories along the way. As we talked to more and more customers, we identified and refined our understanding of their needs and how those needs mapped to different operating segments. We've summarized the highlights of the four operating segments in figure 1–7.

A flu patient, for example, has low-risk and unplanned needs. But when that same patient gets an annual physical exam, a low-risk but planned need, there are very different corresponding priorities for this health-care experience. The variation in the attribute order was not across individual patients or patient demographics, but across the health-care need that prompted a particular visit. And there was incredible convergence within those categories. No matter who was getting treated for the flu, convenience mattered more than coordination of care.

After an initial set of calls, we huddled with the Ochsner executives also working the phones, and we realized that all of the attributes could be broken down into the categories of *before, during,* and *after* the actual delivery of services. There were certain things that patients cared about before they're ever seen by a physician: How long does it take to get an appointment? How long do I wait for the doctor? How far away is the clinic? Then there's their experience during the appointment: Do I feel respected by the doctors and nurses? Did the medical team spend enough time with me, learning about my problem and answering my questions? Did the team solve my problem? The after-appointment considerations consist of billing and follow-up care: Did I get the test results quickly? Was it easy to talk to someone when I didn't understand the bill? Eventually, we developed five attributes within each phase of the service delivery—five before, five during, and five after.

It's important to design a learning process where these types of insights can be revealed. Once you identify your operating segments and measure and compare your performance for each of them, you can start to identify the key drivers of your success or failure. You can see where your organization is winning and losing—and see why those outcomes are entirely predictable.

Again, our recommendation to most clients is this: Go ask your customers what makes them choose you and what makes them choose someone else. Don't guess; ask them. Not surprisingly, our clients then realize that their company is getting business from the operating segments that it is optimized for, whether or not the clients fully understand their own optimization and design choices. When their customers fall into another operating segment (e.g., when these same customers need something done fast), the work goes to someone else. Many people use the U.S. Postal Service regularly for routine mail, but when they need guaranteed, mistake-free delivery, they'll pay a serious premium for FedEx. Same people, two operating segments.

As we mentioned before, if your customers don't all fall in the same operating segment—if they don't all want the same things, in the same order of priority—you have two basic choices. Your first choice is to focus without apology on one operating segment, to build a single service model around one segment's needs and keep your finger on its pulse. That's what Walmart and Southwest do. If a customer outside these companies' core constituency wants to do business with them, Walmart and Southwest will certainly take the money. But the companies won't contort their service models to also meet the needs of these secondary customers.

Your second choice is to build different service models for the operating segments you uncover. Think emergency rooms and outpatient clinics within a single hospital. Or think about the crack service team known as the Geek Squad within Best Buy stores. We'll spend the rest of the book fleshing out the idea of a service model and an entire chapter talking about how to manage multiple models at once, but the visual we want you to have is one organization, many service experiences.

Our most important message here is the need to talk to your customers. A number of perfectly understandable delusions can creep into an executive's basic assumptions. A common one is overconfidence in the value you're delivering, particularly as compared with your competitors. It's easy to rationalize your own service failures—and even easier to see your competitors' flaws in vivid, often caricatured detail. But it's important to stay tethered to reality. Nothing strengthens that connection more than an ongoing dialogue with your customers. Don't outsource this to the marketing department. Don't consume your customers' frustration in sanitized slides delivered by direct reports with little incentive to deliver bad news. Pick up the phone, and confront the truth.

Step 3: Analyze Your Performance

Once you've taken the exercise all the way through this discovery and verification process, it's time to rate the performance of your company relative to your top competitors, with 5 as the highest and 1 as the lowest, and then plot those ratings on the graph. And remember, the rating is from the customer's perspective. How does the customer rate you, and how does the customer rate the competition? The perfect pattern is a nearly diagonal line moving upward from left to right—from 1 to 5—as the categories increase in importance to the customer. Use Walmart and Southwest as your inspiration. The ultimate aim is for the forty-five-degree angle, although companies rarely begin there.

Most companies will discover that they cannot plot themselves at that magical forty-five-degree angle. But the specific pattern they do discover can teach them things about where

FIGURE 1-8

Need a wedge: little difference between your company and competitor

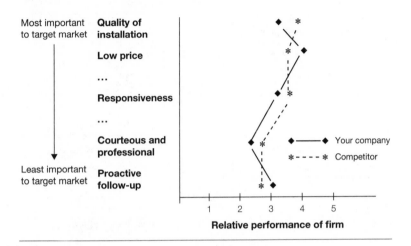

the service model is working and not working. Let's look at some examples of typical pictures and what they mean.

Need a Wedge

If your attribute map looks like the one in figure 1–8 (you're the solid line), essentially there's no difference between you and your competition. You have no meaningful advantage, or wedge, between you and the other players. This is a great place to be a customer, as the customer has all the power. These industries are often marked by low customer loyalty and downward price pressure. Salaries also tend to get stuck, which makes it harder to keep your best people.

Wasted Wedge

The good news (figure 1–9) here is that you have an advantage, but you're getting no return on it. We call it a wasted

FIGURE 1-9

Wasted wedge: investment in attributes that customers don't value

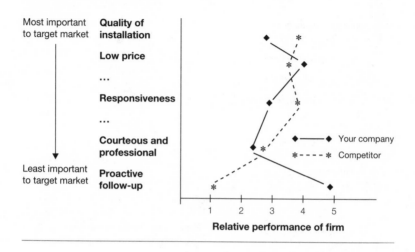

Most important to target market → Least important to target market

- **Quality of installation**
- **Low price**
- ...
- **Responsiveness**
- ...
- **Courteous and professional**
- **Proactive follow-up**

◆———◆ Your company
∗- - - -∗ Competitor

Relative performance of firm
1 2 3 4 5

wedge. You're investing in service features that your customers don't truly value, and it's not translating into profitability or market share. Your decision point: shift resources to attributes your customers value more, or get customers to care more about the things in which you excel. For example, our tap water was fine until bottled water made us want to drink from an obscure Swiss spring.

Wasted Profit

In this scenario (figure 1–10), you're winning on market share, but losing on profitability. You're essentially giving your margin back to your customers in the form of nice-to-have service features that don't change the game or allow you to invest meaningfully in maintaining the sources of real advantage in your industry. Your biggest risk is sustainability.

FIGURE 1-10

Wasted profit: wasting your margin on nice-to-haves

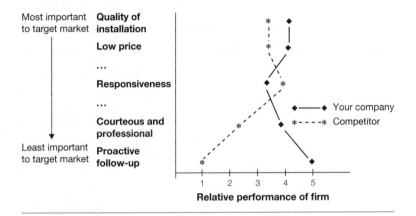

Relative performance of firm

Step 4: React

You've drawn your maps. What now? One obvious response is to shift resources. If you're really good at things that are less important to your customers, then you may be able to re-deploy investment into areas that matter more. Do your core customers care less about innovation and more about how much time they have to wait to get a service rep on site? Table that new R&D initiative, and start adding slack to your service teams.

There is, however, another path to consider as a route to excellence. Some organizations don't simply respond to customer preferences; they actively work to rearrange those preferences. Like the innovators behind bottled water, if they can't win on their customers' existing priorities, they do whatever it takes to change those priorities—to replace or reorder or even eliminate them. That's the story of the Swedish retail phenomenon IKEA.

Redefining Value

In 1943, in a small town in Sweden, seventeen-year-old Ingvar Kamprad started a local catalog company, selling items that were scarce in wartime—things like silk stockings and cigarette lighters—then piggybacking local deliveries onto the milkman's truck. When the war ended, Kamprad invested his consumer insight and scrappy distribution instincts into low-cost home furnishings. By the turn of the century, IKEA had become the world's leading furniture retailer, with more than 300 million people visiting an IKEA store each year.

IKEA's success was built not just on changing the way customers thought about furniture, but on completely reversing their preferences. Customer needs that had long topped the priority list not only dropped down precipitously, but were also replaced by IKEA values that were literally their opposites. IKEA could then take these new attributes, once considered liabilities, and broadcast them as selling points.

As documented beautifully in a case study written by an HBS colleague, Youngme Moon, when IKEA came into the market, physical durability—along with tasteful design that would stand the test of time—were the primary considerations for furniture buyers.[3] According to tradition, young couples would save up for a sober dining room table or couch, then keep that grown-up furniture for decades, sometimes passing it along to their children.

But IKEA's defining offering was flat-pack furniture that came unassembled and was easy to ship, cheap to warehouse, and compact enough for customers to drag home themselves. In the eyes of a disgruntled competitor, this was simply bad furniture that customers had to build. Indeed, some people joked that you could just take it directly from the store to the trash, skipping the middle part, where you set it up in your home. But the market loved it.

And that wasn't the end of IKEA's defiance of tradition. According to the old rules, furniture buying was a solemn rite of passage that required an attentive salesperson to guide you, as well as delivery people to bring the new purchase to your new home, install the new items in their proper place, and even take away your old furniture and dispose of it for you.

IKEA blew up those notions and codified the revolution in its vision statement, which celebrates "Democratic Design" and challenges the customer to "do your part." A customer's job is to pick up the furniture at IKEA's self-service warehouse, drive it home, and then assemble it proudly. And not only is that a reasonable expectation, but it's a better, more empowered way to live.

How did IKEA pull this off? How did it so flagrantly defy "customer needs," not only to survive but also to become the global market leader? The first step was to push well-established attributes downward on the customer's list of preferences. The second was to push the inverse of those attributes up.

There was nothing new about selling cheap furniture. Tables and chairs with thin veneers and components that weren't fastened together properly had always been available. IKEA's innovation was to violate the low-cost-feels-bad assumption. The company called it "Low Price with Meaning," which meant somehow making the purchase and use of inexpensive furniture seem like fun.

With IKEA, cheap didn't mean depressing. Going to IKEA was a good time. Yes, it was a trek to get out to locations where 300,000 square feet of retail space made economic sense, but you were rewarded once you got there. The stores were playful, bright, and modern. IKEA turned the budget experience into a wholesome adventure, like picking your own apples or backpacking in Europe. At the entrance, the store supplied customers with all the tools they'd need for the journey: pencil, paper, tape measures, store maps, as well as the usual shopping carts and strollers. Oh, and a babysitter, too. Each store provided on-site day care for customers. Not even the most expensive furniture maker in the world was offering to watch your kids for you.

And to fuel a full day of empowered consumption, each store had an excellent restaurant that added to the sense of suburban adventure. Instead of the usual big-box mix of vending machines and the rogue hotdog, IKEA's menu included smoked salmon, Swedish meatballs, and lingonberry tarts. Not only did you not feel bad about this low-budget retail experience, but you were affirmed and delighted along the way—which had the added benefit of clearing up any resentment when it took you half a day to assemble a small dresser. The good feelings seemed to linger. As Youngme Moon says, "It's really hard to get mad at someone who gives you an unexpected delight."

And the furniture itself was tasteful and cleverly designed, so you felt far from deprived. It also reflected the modern design revolution (even that toilet brush deserves to be beautiful!), a trend that Target and other retailers would eventually embrace. IKEA caught the wave just as minimalist, Scandinavian design was catching on, and the company rode it with furniture that was sleek and functional and respectful of the human experience.

But IKEA didn't settle for just making you feel better about buying inexpensive furniture that might fall apart in a couple of years. The company managed to frame the furniture's lack of durability as its greatest virtue. This was not just furniture that was fun, but furniture that was, according to IKEA's promotions, "commitment-free." This furniture was so cheap that you could change it almost as easily as you updated your clothes.

The most fundamental—and most radical—new idea from IKEA was that furniture should not be a lifetime investment. And if we're no longer making that kind of commitment, then durability is overrated, right? Who cares about longevity in a world where you get to stop dragging that same old furniture around from year to year? Sick of the sofa? No problem. Lose the baggage and head to IKEA, where you can transform your home and your life. In the brave, new world that IKEA was creating, durability wasn't beside the point; it was an *obstacle.*

Years later, an IKEA executive would be quoted as saying, "It's just furniture. Change it." This sentiment was brought to life in an American ad campaign called "Unboring," with a commercial filmed by Spike Jonze. A woman takes an old lamp out of her apartment and puts in on the curb with the trash. The camera picks up the old lamp's perspective, looking up from the street to the window, where we see the woman installing a nice, new lamp from IKEA. The camera stays with the old lamp on the curb as night falls and it starts to rain. The music picks up the pain of rejection, and we look up to see the woman sitting beside her nice, new lamp in the cozy apartment. Then an actor with a Swedish accent appears out of nowhere, looks directly into the camera and says, "Many of you feel bad for this lamp. That is because you are crazy. It has no feelings. And the new one is much better."

IKEA knew it couldn't win within the usual conventions of the retail furniture business. IKEA found itself rated 1 on each of its target customers' leading attributes: durability, ease of assembly, sales assistance, and location of the retail outlet (figure 1–11).

And so the retailer remade the list (figure 1–12). With IKEA's help, target customers now had a new list of attributes for furniture buying:

• The ability to change

• The joy of redecorating whenever you feel like it

FIGURE 1-11

Attribute map for IKEA

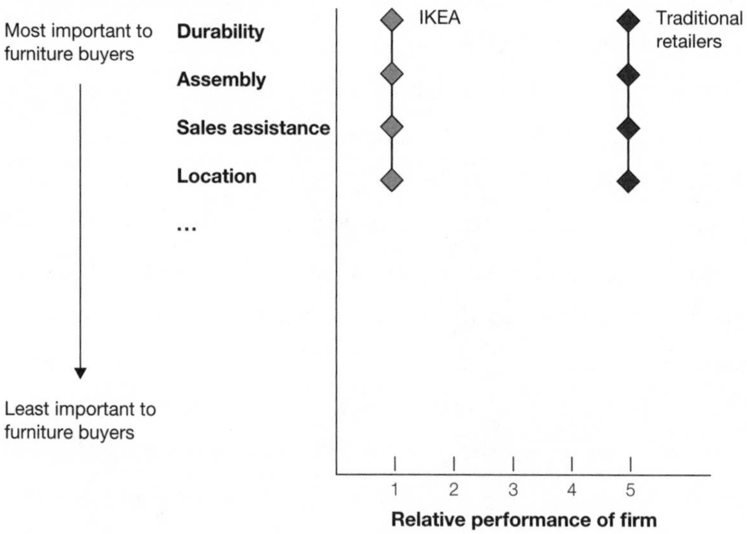

FIGURE 1-12

Remade attribute map for IKEA

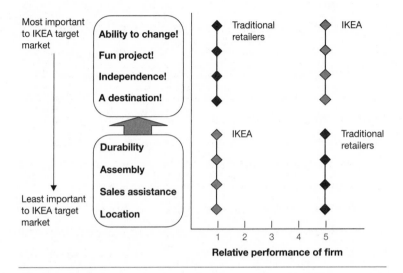

- The freedom to live without the emotional baggage and sunk costs of traditional furnishings

- A destination retail experience, the perfect family outing for a blustery Saturday afternoon

IKEA achieved what few companies have achieved, but what we believe is a powerful model: the company changed its customers' relationship with the category. It reordered its customers' attribute list, and then some.

Corporate Blinders

Finally, let's check back in on Commerce Bank. In 2007, Toronto Dominion (TD) bought the company for $8.5 billion, and its performance postmerger didn't live up to the bankers' analytics. The gap speaks to the importance of understanding the true drivers of service excellence.

By our read, Toronto Dominion's well-intentioned bankers understood financial models but not service models. They saw that Commerce had a high cost structure (from those extended hours and service perks) and a low cross-sell, and the new owners got to work right away improving both metrics. But Toronto Dominion didn't realize that the "weaknesses" they'd diagnosed in Commerce's financial statements were there by design—or that these attributes, in fact, represented critical ingredients in the happy bank's secret sauce.

No sign of the intricate set of trade-offs that drove Commerce's success was easily identifiable on its balance sheet. The idea of 1's and 5's, of supporting excellence in the areas that matter most by sacrificing the areas that matter least—this is not easily captured by financial statements. Imagine a Commerce employee doing a currency swap. Better yet, imagine yourself as the customer in line behind the customer trying to get the currency swap. The employee struggles, you the customer no longer experience the excellent service offering you've come to expect, and the entire system breaks down.

Preventing this outcome requires organizations with deep intuition about the links between finance and service operations. We call these firms *bilingual*, and they're surprisingly rare. Which may be why, at last report, Vernon Hill has started the first new retail bank in London in over a century.[4]

UNCOMMON TAKEAWAYS

✓ To achieve service excellence, you must underperform in strategic ways. This means delivering on the service dimensions your customers value most, and then making it possible—profitable and sustainable—by performing poorly on the dimensions they value least. In other words, you must be bad in the service of good.

✓ The primary obstacle to service excellence is not the ambition to be great, but the stomach to be bad. This is an emotional obstacle.

✓ It's difficult to compete without understanding your customers' needs and how well your competitors are meeting those needs. Fortunately, customers are typically very willing to give you that information. And it's cheap and easy to ask them for it.

✓ There is an important distinction between marketing and operating segments. Marketing segments tell us how to identify and communicate with different kinds of customers. Operating segments tell us how to *serve* customers differently. There is rarely a one-to-one mapping between these segments.

✓ There are two key ways to improve service: (1) meet your customers' existing needs more effectively, or (2) convince your customers that they need something you already do well.

✓ There is a difference between financial models and service models. Service companies need to be "bi-lingual" to excel.

Chapter Two

Truth Number 2: Someone Has to Pay for It

In 2003, in an increasingly competitive marketplace, Celebrity Cruises launched an initiative called 150 Tastes of Luxury. The initiative added additional service improvements to Celebrity's premium cruise experience.

For more than a decade, Celebrity had been known for great service and exceptional cuisine, but this offering took these amenities to the next level. A holiday mood was set the moment the passenger stepped on board. Customers were greeted on deck with a chilled glass of champagne and delighted by new "tastes" everywhere they turned: cold towels and fresh sorbet poolside, sunset yoga and Pilates, expanded dining options that included sushi cafés and pasta and pizza bars. Shortly after introducing the program, Celebrity raised the bar even higher with Concierge Class, which included additional amenities such as an offering it called Acupuncture at Sea.

The people loved it, but here's the question: would they pay for it?

Celebrity customers adored being handed champagne—your customers probably would, too—but would they reward Celebrity for the gesture with increased revenues? Or is this an example of what we call *gratuitous service,* service nice-to-haves donated to customers, with little chance of recovering their costs?

Funding Greatness

The most successful service models incorporate a mechanism for reliably funding an exceptional experience. Without a reliable funding source designed directly into the model, organizations risk delivering service that customers happily consume but never pay for. In our experience, four funding mechanisms can be used to sustain your premium offering—and only one of them requires that you charge premium prices. Said another way, there are four ways to pay for excellence:

1. Charge customers extra for it—in a palatable way.

2. Make cost reductions that also improve service.

3. Make service improvements that also reduce costs.

4. Get customers to do the work for you.

Funding Source 1: When Customers Are Happy to Pay More

The first of these mechanisms—getting the customer to pay extra—sounds straightforward enough, at least at first blush.

Recall the Hotel Cipriani, which passes along the cost of an exceptional service experience by charging 50 percent more than its nearest competitor. But that option is out of reach for the vast majority of businesses, including Celebrity Cruises. Most markets won't tolerate such a large price premium.

Complicating matters for Celebrity was that cruise travel is primarily booked through travel agents, even for repeat business. Customers rely on agents, who often assign little distinction among cruise experiences. Customers take their pick from a short list of cruise packages that all sound similar, and so the lowest-priced option typically wins. Most cruise customers are already price sensitive, and this dynamic exacerbates price competition. As a result, it's almost impossible to translate a Celebrity customer's delight into a willingness to pay a higher price. And so Celebrity had a very difficult time getting paid for 150 Tastes of Luxury.

Celebrity's customers weren't likely to pay for extra service, at least not in the way it was presented. But there are creative ways around these constraints in almost every industry. Recall Commerce Bank's funding source—rather than charge customers outright for better service, Commerce offered an interest rate on deposits that was half a percentage point *lower* than the rate the competition was paying. Customers essentially paid for the service every day, whether they used it or not. In contrast, attempts to charge extra for visits to the teller often fail miserably. It just seems unfair to pay extra to talk to someone about your own money. Even when customers would be economically better off by being charged per teller visit, most still perceive it as wrong. The half a percentage point hit doesn't feel as bad. We call this *palatable pricing*.

The more palatable the pricing, the more you can charge. Said differently, the less palatable the pricing, the more irritated customers tend to get over every penny extracted from them. In personal investing, when you rely on a broker instead of E*TRADE, you pay higher transaction fees. But you don't pay extra for phone calls and meetings, even though those interactions are among the most valuable parts of the service experience. That's the deal. You pay a lot for each stock trade, which covers the broker's time—at no additional charge—to talk you down when the market tanks.

Similarly, a large part of the appeal of Starbucks is that you can linger all afternoon or evening over a single latte. We've known people who have started companies, fallen in love, and stayed sane in their child's first few months on the planet, all from their favorite corner Starbucks table. It makes a $3 cup of coffee sound like a bargain. Indeed, the assumption that you'll stick around is factored into the premium price you pay for the beverages. It is an explicit and transparent value proposition going in, but you won't find any meters next to those comfortable stuffed chairs.

The Fury over Airline Fees

But the definition of a "palatable" can vary widely. In 2008, with fuel prices headed through the ceiling, most major airlines started charging for "extras." In some cases, an extra meant anything beyond a place to sit and a supply of oxygen. Checking a bag was no longer part of the basic transportation contract, but rather an opportunity to collect a fee. Fees for a pillow or a blanket followed, as well as charges for soft drinks. Customers largely put up with it, although the grumbling was starting to build. When US Airways started charging for bottled water, the airline discovered that it had overstepped. The grumbling turned into fighting back, and the movement for passengers' rights was born. US Airways flight attendants were suddenly confronted with irate customers. Within six months, the airline had to back off and return to hydrating its passengers for free.

Customer reactions can be unpredictable—and visceral. In the moment when airline fees exploded, Southwest, alone among the major carriers, maintained the position that customers would rather have pricing that was palatable and transparent. As documented widely in the business press, "freedom from fees" became a badge of honor and a banner on the Southwest Web site.[1]

Southwest's customers rejoiced. But the story isn't so simple—take a look around the airline industry, and you'll see that a fees-for-perks strategy works for some carriers but not others. Spirit Air, a European carrier, unapologetically charges for everything. What makes the difference?

The difference between a palatable charge and a customer rebellion seems to come down to the contract that originally engaged the customer. A central part of what Southwest is delivering is captured in its LUV logo, which is also its stock ticker symbol. When your friends at Southwest charge you extra for small things, they're violating the terms of the relationship. It's like your mother charging you rent for your bedroom.

Spirit Air, in contrast, is not trying to be your friend. The company's deal is this—we're practically giving you the flight, so suck it up and don't complain. At Spirit Air, the idea of paying for a checked bag seems fair, largely because you're starting off with a ticket price that can be as low as $9. It's the same customer contract at easyJet, another super discount carrier, where the founder's vision was to "make flying as affordable as buying a pair of jeans." This vision extends to all easyJet services. At the affiliated easyHotel, you may have to pay extra for a clean towel, but when the room itself costs $19, that feels reasonable.

Which is not to say that customers find nothing to complain about at discounters. In 2008, Spirit Air had by far the most complaints in the industry. But Spirit Air customers weren't provoked by the predictable deprivations. They weren't shocked when they had to pay extra for a soft drink, but complained bitterly when they were hit with charges they didn't expect and that didn't seem fair. Ninety percent of Spirit Air tickets are purchased online, for example, and it wasn't until after your credit card was charged that you were asked if you wanted to select a seat or check a bag. If you consumed these "extras," your card was charged again. For seat selection, in particular, customers felt as if they had been duped. The lesson? Transparency matters when it comes to pricing—it's part of the palatability calculus—and it matters even more if you're competing on a straight-up, no-frills, adult-to-adult relationship with your customers.

Palatable pricing depends heavily on the deal you're making with your customers. At US Airways, the expectations for customer care are much higher than at a discount carrier, mainly because the ticket price is higher. As a result, bag fees are a source of incessant complaints. Further complicating things is that customers on the same flight with the same level of service can pay vastly different prices for their ticket. Indeed, customers might pay anywhere from $200 to $1,000 to fly from Boston to Washington, but regardless of whether you spent $200 or $1,000, you get stuck with the same fee for that extra bag. The incongruity doesn't sit well.

The Four Seasons hotels made the same mistake at its flagship Manhattan location, where the hotel charged guests extra for wireless Internet access, even though some of them were paying thousands of dollars a night for the room. It just felt bad to have to dig out your credit card for a $19.99 fee while sitting in an I. M. Pei–designed room.

Local governments, at a time of radically decreased tax revenues, are also testing their market's tolerance for fees to not only raise service levels, but also to keep basic services alive. The mayor of Washington, D.C., has proposed a streetlight user fee to be added to every electric bill. New York City has started slapping a $100 fine on anyone dropping off the kids at school and leaving the engine running for more than a minute. Fees for dog licenses and other nominal fees have gone up everywhere, and some municipalities have toyed with the idea of charging their "guests" for spending a night in jail.

But the fees that tend to infuriate citizens are those that seem to violate some basic notion of a fair exchange. The most provocative proposal in civic circles is the accident-response fee for police and fire. Citizens think of these first responders as the good guys, their heroes in a time of need—not to mention providers of basic services that taxpayers assume they've already paid for. For this reason, people are outraged when the bill for two police cruisers arrives a couple of weeks after a car accident.

The point is that if you do charge extra, then you also have to make sure that the charge is easy to digest. When customers feel as though you've violated your agreement with them—that you've been unfair or misleading or simply petty—you risk a lot more than lost revenue. You risk losing the market's trust, the foundation of the enterprise.

The Truth About Loyalty Programs

Loyalty programs—designed correctly—are a great way to get paid for your premium service. Unfortunately, too many of these programs are simply paying their customers, through discounts, to stick around. Companies stick a loyalty label on a thinly veiled customer-retention program.

Here's the definition of a true loyalty program: you provide additional service features to your best customers—say, invite them to special events or give them access to company leadership. In return, their commitment to your brand and willingness to pay for services go up. Nothing gratuitous here.

As documented recently in the *Wall Street Journal,* the loyalty program offered by the European grocer Asda is an excellent—and rare—illustration of a true loyalty program.[a] Asda is involving its loyal customers in strategic decisions such as which products to offer and how these items should be arranged in the store. Some customers will get early access to products so that their opinions will have more influence. Good customers will effectively earn the right to be a part of the company's decision making, to make the stores more responsive to their own individual needs. As we'll discuss later in the book, these customers will help to coproduce the service they eventually consume.

But most organizations don't take Asda's approach. Instead, they create a customer retention (or acquisition) program and then mistakenly call it a loyalty program. When companies pay customers through discounts to remain customers, it's a customer retention program. When companies pay customers to try out their products and services, it's a customer acquisition program. When companies invest in activities that increase customers' willingness to pay a premium price, then they have a loyalty program. A successful loyalty program increases the chance that your customers will choose you over a lower-priced competitor. The confusion of terms wouldn't be a big deal, except that a mislabeled loyalty program can get in the way of creating a real one.

Grocers on both sides of the Atlantic have been touting their loyalty cards for years, with Tesco claiming the largest one. These are effectively retention programs, where customers earn future discounts based on their current purchase behavior. Companies like Tesco are essentially bribing their customers to remain customers. This is a classic retention tactic.

In contrast, Asda's customers are improving the company's service and become more devoted to the brand along the way. Everybody wins. And if some of these customers turn out to be very helpful, Asda has committed to compensate them accordingly. If a member of its loyalty program comes up with an idea that saves the business money, that customer will receive 5 percent of the value of the first year's savings—say, $100,000 on $2 million in savings.

No one else in the industry is making these kinds of deals with its customers—or getting rewarded for its effort in the same way.

a. Lilly Vitorovich, "Grocer Asda Turns to Customers for Advice," *Wall Street Journal*, October 2, 2009, http://online.wsj.com/article/SB 125440249562856121.html.

Funding Source 2: When Reducing Costs Improves Service

Sometimes, cost reductions that also improve service are so familiar we hardly notice them. The classroom or seminar, with the chance to exchange ideas and learn from other students, is a better way of learning than private instruction, but the classroom model was developed because it was more cost-efficient than private tutors. In some cases, group therapy provides the same kinds of benefits—clients learn from their peers and get inspired by their courage and progress—and the cost of service delivery is dramatically reduced.

Lower Costs, Better Service at Progressive Insurance

A less intuitive example of what's possible can be found in the auto insurance industry. This industry has a few peculiarities about it. First, firms tend to lose money on the provision of insurance. That is, firms tend to pay out more in claims than they bring in through premiums. How do they survive? Because customers pay in advance and the investment gains from prepaid premiums cover the loss and provide a small profit. Thus, an innovation we'd be unlikely to see in this industry is that customers no longer have to pay in advance—the prepay arrangement is what's funding the whole thing. A second interesting observation about this industry is just how price-sensitive it is. If one insurance company is even a few dollars cheaper than another, customers tend to flock to it.

With these constraints in mind, consider Progressive Insurance, a company that spends more on service than other firms, yet its customers don't pay extra for it. How is this possible? Because the service improvements reduce costs dramatically, which more than covers the expense of providing the additional service.

When a Progressive client has an auto accident, the company deploys an immediate-response van to assist the client in distress, often arriving on the scene before the police or tow trucks. A clean, crisp Progressive employee comes to save the day, dusts off the customer, and asks all the right emotionally intelligent questions. The empathetic employee then assesses the damage and often cuts the customer a check *on the spot,* not days or weeks after the accident.

To be clear, this is not inexpensive. The branded, four-wheel-drive trucks; the wireless technology to know how much to settle the claim for; the managing of three shifts of claims adjusters because customers don't get into accidents along the traditional work hours of nine to five—all of it costs real money.

How can Progressive afford it in such a price-sensitive industry? Just like Celebrity Cruises passengers, Progressive customers love the service but are unlikely to pay more for it. But immediate-response vans aren't gratuitous service. It turns out that the insurance industry is ripe with fraud, and a clever way to combat fraud is to show up at the scene of an accident and observe firsthand what actually happened. Internally, Progressive has been known to refer to its trucks as fraud-busters, and they do exactly what the name suggests.

Progressive's on-site service model has other cost advantages, too. The insurance industry is also rife with legal claims, but Progressive learned that if an adjuster arrives at the scene of an accident and asks the customer, "Are you OK?" then that customer is much less likely to involve a lawyer. The experience has the effect of humanizing the insurance company and diffusing a customer's anger, which makes Progressive less of a target. By simply caring enough to ask, Progressive reduces its clients' interest in suing.

Fraud, disputed claims, and legal fees represent $15 out of every $100 in insurance premiums across the industry. But when a claims adjuster shows up within minutes with a sharp eye and an open heart, both fraud and legal costs tumble. By drastically lowering these operating costs, Progressive's excellence more than pays for itself.

The kind of innovation represented by Progressive's immediate-response vans requires a specific sequence. Progressive started out by targeting its biggest buckets of cost—fraud, disputed claims, and legal fees—and then worked out from there to find ways to dress up the cost savings as value-added service. This is the secret to the second funding mechanism: sequence matters. Start with costs.

Progressive has continued to innovate in ways like this. Another unwieldy cost category for the auto insurance industry has been reimbursements to independent auto repair shops. These shops delivered uneven quality for a wide range of prices, and insurers felt helpless in maintaining control over them. So Progressive began to coordinate the activities among a much smaller group of repair shops, where experience and scale could be leveraged—and improved the customer experience along the way. Progressive now offers customers an optional concierge level of claims service in which it will arrange for the customers' cars to be repaired after an accident. This removes a great deal of hassle for customers, who would typically have to find a repair shop, navigate the reimbursement policy, and hope they get decent value for the money they're spending. Progressive handles all of these steps for the customer, saving them time and anxiety. And the company does it all without charging anything extra, because of the savings generated by using a smaller set of repair shops with which Progressive has built reliable relationships. These savings more than pay for the added value to the customer.

One way that Progressive has continued to innovate is by defining the concept of service improvements broadly. In this brutally price-sensitive industry, Progressive now provides customers with a comparison quote, a helpful quote for its service alongside the quotes for all its major competitors. Now customers don't need to waste their time shopping around— Progressive does it for them. And when Progressive's quote isn't the lowest, customers go to the competition.

At first glance, this seems like an unusual thing to do, particularly since Progressive is the lowest only about half the time, thus funneling inquiries to its competitors at a healthy clip. But the insurer is using the comparison quote as a way to select customers.

Progressive is widely considered one of the industry's best at the underlying analytics of insurance. It invested in this advantage at its inception, when it exclusively served high-risk drivers, a diverse segment it believed was being inappropriately priced by the market. These customers require superior analysis to price effectively, and Progressive became very good at it, very quickly. While Progressive continued to benefit from its superior assessments—in evaluating any customer, not just the high-risk ones—it finally really monetized this advantage when it created the comparison quote.

Consider figure 2–1, where the true riskiness of a customer is represented by the vertical axis, and the premium charged by Progressive's competitors is represented by the horizontal axis. If the competition were perfect at pricing risk—something that is certainly not true—then the customers on this graph would be lined up on a forty-five-degree angle.

With this backdrop, consider two customers calling Progressive for a comparison quote. Customer A calls—someone

FIGURE 2-1

Progressive Insurance strategy for its comparison quotes

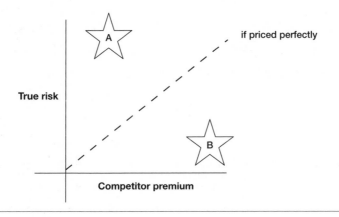

who represents high risk and whom the competition is under-charging. Progressive gives A its own quote and quotes for its nearest competitors. Since Progressive will not be the lowest quote, A will choose the competition. This is a positive outcome for Progressive, as it contributes to its competitors' losing money on insurance. It's a different story for customer B, a low-risk customer whom the competition is essentially overcharging. In this case, Progressive will be the lowest price, acquire the customer, and still make a profit. The comparison quote lets Progressive select its target customers—in a format that is widely valued by the industry's price-sensitive customers.

Again, note the value of this latest innovation: while Progressive was always better at risk assessment, not until it put some teeth into its value proposition—until it built a service offering on top of that proposition—did the company fully realize the benefit of its operational strengths.

Funding Source 3: When Improving Service Lowers Costs

There's another way to achieve the same goal of better service and lower costs. As Jim Heskett, Earl Sasser, and Len Schlesinger described in their breakthrough book on service, *The Service Profit Chain*, Intuit founder Scott Cook increased the cost and quality of the customer service he was delivering in order to reduce the unpaid demand for it.[2] To Cook, providing outstanding phone support to users of his small-business software—the bane of most call centers—could be a useful source of input for continued product development and ultimately a cost-reduction strategy. So Intuit asked its product development team to suit up with headsets and field calls.

When Intuit customers called up for live software support, they were likely to get someone who understood the product's functionality better than anyone else on the planet, an engineer who had been charged with product improvement and who may have played a role in designing the software. This was a sharp departure from the service experience offered by many other software providers, which provided phone support through an outsourced customer service team with tight scripts and a relatively superficial understanding of product features.

Cook's logic was this—what better way to gain firsthand knowledge of where users are stumbling? This was information that could be used to make subsequent versions of Intuit products more intuitive—and reduce the need for customers to pick up the phone in the first place. "Our competitors think we're crazy," Cook told some HBS colleagues, "but if we got as many calls as they did, we'd be out of business."[3] The investment has paid off in better software, which means lower call volume, which allows for better service and lower tech-support costs down the road.

The point here is that improving service in one part of your business can substantially lower costs elsewhere—thereby funding the premium experience. At Zappos, the giant online shoe retailer, the cost of providing over-the-top service is considered the cost of building the brand. "We can spend money on shipping and sales fulfillment, or we can spend more on marketing," chief financial officer Alfred Lin told us in a recent interview. "Our view is that this money is fungible."

We visited the Zappos Las Vegas headquarters in 2009, and CEO Tony Hsieh spelled out the company's approach more explicitly:

> *We view most of the money that we put into the customer experience as our marketing dollars. The number one driver of our business is repeat customers and word of mouth, so most of the money that we would have spent on paid advertising we put toward things like free shipping both ways, surprise upgrades to overnight shipping, our call center, and our warehouse, which we run twenty-four/seven—which isn't actually the most efficient way to run the warehouse. The most efficient way is to let the orders pile up, but because we run it twenty-four/seven to get our orders out as quickly as possible, customers can order as late as midnight Eastern [time], and it is on their doorstep eight hours later. That creates that "Wow!" effect, and they remember that for a long time. And then they tell their friends.*

Sure, Zappos does a few other things to fund the exceptional service it provides, such as finding innovative ways to reduce the cost of inventory management. The retailer also simply charges customers palatably for the extra attention, in the form of higher-priced shoes. But it's the steep reduction in marketing costs that really fuels the premium experience. Zappos service has made such an impression that the company doesn't need to invest in spreading the word. Its customers already can't stop talking about it.

Avoiding the Curse of Free Riders: Gateway versus Amazon

When the PC company Gateway, Inc., decided to expand from an online model to physical stores, it chose to compete on a magnificent prepurchase service experience. Customers could wander into Gateway stores and gain a full education on the ins and outs of PC buying, from highly skilled salespeople in beautiful, strategically sited (read: expensive) retail locations that facilitated healthy foot traffic. The minute a potential customer strolled into the store, an attentive salesperson would appear gracefully at his or her side to deliver a customized personal tutoring session on The Right Computer for You. Customers loved it. And then they'd go home and order the right Dell for them at two-thirds the price.

Why could Dell and other Gateway competitors pull this off? They could charge lower prices because they didn't have to pay for expensive stores staffed by expensive employees. And because their products were considered indistinguishable by the market, Dell et al. could effectively outsource the customer education function to Gateway. Gateway created a situation that was ripe for free riding. When there is high utility of information prepurchase and ease of substitution among products—as there is with PCs—you run a real risk that your investment in service excellence will walk across the street and give its money to a competitor. Your customers will not stick around out of gratitude. That's what Gateway discovered when it opened—and rather quickly closed—hundreds of retail stores.

Amazon should be facing an onslaught of customer free riding. Its products are rarely the lowest-priced option, and they're very easy to substitute—indeed, Amazon's competitors sell exactly the same things. Many products also benefit from the vast amounts of up-front information loaded onto the site, including product specs, manufacturers' descriptions, and hundreds of thoughtfully culled customer reviews. How does Amazon pull it off? By making the pivot from prepurchase to purchase as seamless and lovely as possible.

Amazon saves credit card, shipping, and billing information and even has a patented one-click shopping mechanism that dramatically reduces the time from intent to actual purchase. This purchase functionality makes it irresistibly easy, once you've found what you're looking for, to point and click and be done with it. And because it's so easy, Amazon gets to avoid Gateway's fate. Amazon can invest heavily in prepurchase functionality without losing its customers to the competition.

Amazon essentially wins on ease of use. This becomes increasingly important when the alternative supplier is competing on price. Buy.com's business model is to be cheaper than Amazon, but the value proposition does not support either the prepurchase or the purchase functionality that Amazon provides. If you know exactly what you're looking for, you can buy it cheaper at Buy.com. But if you're browsing or have imperfect information, you can find a product a lot more easily on Amazon. Buy.com is positioning for Amazon free riders—customers who will rely on Amazon's incredible computer system for research, then close the deal at Buy.com or some other, low-cost alternative. But Amazon is making its customers *very comfortable* staying right where they are.

Funding Source 4: When Customers Serve Themselves

The method for funding service with the longest, if spottiest pedigree is getting customers to work for free, rather than paying those high-cost employees. Self-service food shopping led the way in 1916, in Memphis, when an enterprising grocer named Clarence Saunders introduced the concept to his Piggly Wiggly stores. Before then, even though the grocery store "chain" was in full bloom, with brands like Kroger and A&P,

goods were stored in barrels or bags, and customers relied on a clerk behind a counter to collect each item for them.

Saunders's innovation, which he tried to patent as the "self-serving store," essentially opened up the stockroom to customers. And even though it required much more work on the part of the customers, the concept was a huge success. Customers loved the greater access, selection, and control over their service experience. Now shoppers could read labels, compare prices, and examine each object themselves—and take their sweet time doing it.

In the years that followed, the idea of self-service was married to the concept of the chain store, and the supermarket was born. It launched a wave of innovation geared toward the self-service customer. In 1937, the first wheeled shopping cart was introduced. Three years later, the first doors with an electric eye opened automatically. In the 1970s, the big innovation was the bar code scanner, which reduced wait times for all those self-servers and led to the 1996 denouement—fully automated, self-service checkout lanes. This is where the engine of self-service innovation in food retail stalled.

Self-service checkout at the supermarket is currently problematic for the simple reason that shoppers receive little if any benefit for their effort. They are doing the extra set of tasks that an employee would do, without getting anything in return for their labor. For self-service to be part of service excellence, this option must be so good that it's preferred to a *readily available* full-service alternative. It is a flawed test to compare self-service with an unappealing, full-service alternative, for example, a staffed checkout aisle with a twenty-minute line.

The irony of self-service checkout in grocery stores is that many executives consider it a success because of the increased traffic at the self-service registers. Look closer, however, and you'll see that the increased traffic comes from reducing the number of employees attending to full-service checkout aisles, which makes it all but impossible to get through some stores without performing the checkout function yourself. Look even closer, and you'll see beads of sweat forming on the foreheads of customers in these lines, as their anxiety builds as they try to get the bar code scanner to work and read complicated instructions on the small screens in front of them. Forget the empowerment of filling your own cart and indulging your quirky preferences in blissful solitude. Self-service in today's grocery store is a cost-saving strategy that intimidates and exhausts the customer. And is unlikely to leave anyone better off.

This is not such an uncommon service model. Many businesses try to save money by asking customers to do extra work. But most models—such as self-service gas pumps—have the courtesy to pay customers for their effort in the form of a meaningful discount. They also carry few illusions that this route leads to service excellence.

When excellence is the goal, you must make customers better off along the way. The airline industry offers a very clean example of self-service innovation that creates real value for consumers. Airlines confronted precisely the same dilemma facing supermarkets—the need for an automated self-service alternative—but they have figured out how to make it work. The reason: an airline's best customers *prefer* check-in kiosks to dealing with an employee tapping away behind the counter.

The majority of frequent fliers prefer the kiosks because they're fast and easy to use and provide better functionality than the full-service alternative. Check-in kiosks give the airline passenger more control over the service experience, primarily through the seat-selection chart. That simple graphical depiction of the plane, demonstrating which seats are available and which are taken, gives customers far more information and control than any amount of back-and-forth with a full-service agent and a black-box computer system. No longer do you have to explain to a uniformed stranger why your stomach staple makes an aisle seat a travel imperative for you. At a kiosk, you can maintain some dignity and quietly, graciously, meet your own needs.

Let's revisit that agent's black-box computer, because there's an important self-service principal here. Try to recall the last time a full-service airline agent helped you with anything. How hard did he or she have to work on the other side of the counter? We once peeked over to get a look at the action. Sure enough, systems and screens and codes we couldn't begin to understand were whizzing by as the agent's fingers flew over the keyboard. If the airlines simply gave us access to that system, we'd never be able to serve ourselves. It would be far too complicated. But the airlines were smart and transformed the complicated system aimed at trained employees into a simple system that could be handled by customers. A touch screen seat map creates superior value that is delightfully easy for customers to consume.

Again, contrast this experience with the stressful design of the self-service grocery checkout. Self-serving food shoppers are being asked to perform the same tasks that one or more trained clerks normally perform—finding the little bar code, scanning it quickly, bagging items without breaking any eggs. In addition, some stores have even added steps. Their customers have to do *more* work than their employees once did, like complicated maneuvers to weigh packages as part of a fraud-detection program. Grocery stores made the checkout job more difficult for customers, and the predictable outcome is that customers don't like it.

How Much Extra Are You Charging for Self-Service?

Some sushi bars in Asia now have a touch screen system that allows the customer to order directly from the chef. Certain emergency rooms have facilitated self-service admission with a touch screen diagram of the human body. You simply touch the digital body part that's giving you trouble. With further advances in technology, supermarkets still have the chance to get it right. Radio-frequency identification tags should soon enable supermarkets to do away with checkout entirely. You'll be able to put a product in your shopping cart, and the transaction would be recorded and complete. That's self-service that customers would prefer, which is the only kind that leads to excellence.

Here's the real goal—can you create a self-service solution that is so good that your customers would pay more for it?

Consider the salad bar, perhaps the most iconic example of consumers meeting their own service needs. The salad bar has found a permanent place in our food culture because it offers a service enhancement that millions of people, at least some of the time, prefer. There's much to be said for the ability to customize your order from a wide variety of options and build precisely the salad you want. Fire and Ice, a premium restaurant chain launched in the Boston area, extends this concept to the entrée as well. You pick the portion of meat or fish that you want, watch while the chef grills it, then customize the rest of your order by request. Despite the money it saves by not flooding the floor with attentive waitstaff, Fire and Ice is not competing on lower prices. It's competing as a fun, interactive destination, offering a dining experience that is truly distinct. The restaurant is charging its customers for the privilege of meeting their own needs. That's the idea.

Putting It into Practice

From a design perspective, charging extra (see "Funding Source 1," earlier in the chapter) is the simplest way to fund uncommon service. But many markets won't tolerate the price premium required to cover the cost of delivering excellence. And so you typically need to get creative. Whenever we consult with managers in search of a funding source, we tend to skip past the idea of charging higher prices in exchange for better service. If you can pull it off, go for it, but we're unlikely to be of much use in the brainstorming. You know better than we do what your customers will stomach.

Instead, we jump right to the more complex strategies, the last three funding sources on our list: cost reductions that improve service, service improvements that reduce costs, and self-service that feels right—so right that customers will pay more for it.

Step 1: Examine Your Cost Structure

The place to begin your search for ways to fund uncommon service is with your biggest buckets of costs, which often represent your biggest buckets of potential savings. (When people get stuck here, we suggest starting by reducing the *time* involved in a customer-facing process. This will often yield better experiences at a lower cost to the organization.)

For example, the owner of a chain of supermarkets once told us that his biggest bucket of cost is legal liability. The cost of insurance increases with the number of people who slip and fall. This is a win-win in the making. Find strategies that make your stores safer and that will also enhance the service experience, and you will bring down your premiums. If the risk of a fall is higher for patrons over seventy-five, maybe these customers could have access to an employee who would help them shop (and avoid possible injury). Or maybe you could introduce a new service where customers can submit an order online and store runners shop for them, which reduces the number of distracted parents rushing around the retail space, trying to grab a gallon of milk and still pick the kids up from school on time. This is how the exercise works.

CASE STUDY

FedEx

FedEx took the idea of improving service while lowering costs to heart in its IT strategy. The company had a cost driver that was screaming for attention—the "where's my order?" call. The industry economics are such that if a company has to handle one of these calls with a live agent, it loses money on that package. Each time a customer phones in to track a package, the company experiences a loss. FedEx knew it had to find a way to cut back on the number of calls, but it approached cost reduction as a search for improved service. How could the company reduce these costs while simultaneously improving the service experience?

First, FedEx allowed customers to track their packages online. One immediate advantage in providing online access is that it enables both company and client to cut and paste the sixteen-digit code used to track the 650,000 FedEx packages that go flying around the world each day. Having someone at a call center read that number out to the customer, or vice versa, is problematic enough, even before you factor in the multiple ways that spoken English can be accented. But the real revolution was the company's next move—automating and proactively sending tracking information by e-mail or text (whichever the customer prefers) so that no one ever needs to wonder and certainly never needs to call. FedEx set out to reduce costs and ended up making customers much better off. With the old system, customers had to proactively call to check on the status of a shipment. Now everyone can rest easy knowing that FedEx is on top of it.[a]

Even when things inevitably go wrong. FedEx innovated again with *exception reporting,* alerts that let customers know about the infrequent cases in which a FedEx package is going to be late. Again, these alerts eliminate the need for anyone to pick up the phone, reducing both customer anxiety and company costs. Again, FedEx is on it. Sorry for screw-up, but we're on it—

we're giving you better information, at a faster rate and much lower cost than staffing a high-service call center.

a. Airlines took the same cue when they started sending out automated, proactive updates for passengers on upcoming flights. These automated calls and e-mails anticipate what the passenger wants to know—for example, whether a flight is delayed or a gate has been changed—and provide the information in advance, saving the airline the trouble and expense of responding to individual inquiries.

Step 2: Monetize Your Strengths

In addition to looking at your largest cost drivers, ask yourselves, "What can we do better than anyone else?" That is, beyond the rhetoric of annual reports and marketing collateral, what makes you really and truly superior? Start here, and think about a value-added service that allows you to benefit operationally from your excellence—bonus if you can make your competition uncomfortable along the way.

For example, in trying to help a security company redesign its service model, we asked company leaders where the company stood in the competitive landscape. The CEO said that his main competition was the national firms, and so his distinctive edge was in being local. So then we asked how, specifically, the customer benefited from the firm's location. And could this also be an area for cost advantages? He responded that customers benefited because his company really understood them. We asked how that manifested explicitly, and we discovered that being local was indeed a point of pride for the company but not necessarily benefiting its customers or cost structure in a tangible way. It was a nice talking point, but it had little substance. So the challenge was to put teeth into the value proposition, to really deliver on the idea that being local was an advantage. With this frame, it took very little time to realize that a time-sensitive on-site guarantee would be cost-prohibitive to the national players and relatively easy for this company to deliver and defend.

Interestingly, the obstacle to innovation at this company was its confidence that it was already capitalizing on its strengths. As soon as its managers had the courage to acknowledge the gap between chatter and truth—between what they were vaguely promising and what they were explicitly delivering—we were able to make progress in relatively short order.

The security company is not alone in this. We often find the obstacle to innovation is an unwillingness to acknowledge reality, including the hard truth that you're not creating the value you claim to be creating. Once we establish that there's more to be done, the brainstorming is often fast and furious. Without that acknowledgment, however, organizations can retreat to a defensive and reluctant crouch.

Step 3: Unleash Your Customers

The move to self-service is usually a cost-cutting initiative. But as we've discussed, it's not enough to just cut costs. Again, the goal here is self-service that's so good that you can cut costs while raising prices. When we ask organizations how much extra they charge for self-service, they often look at us as if we're crazy.

"We charge nothing—if anything, we offer a discount for it."

At which point, we clarify that they're not done innovating.

Ochsner Health System recently began experimenting with patient portals for its Baton Rouge clinic. The portals allow clients to serve a range of their own needs online, from refilling prescriptions to receiving lab results to scheduling their own appointments right into a physician's schedule. The results? Adoption rates are high, and patient feedback is very positive. The initiative is part of a larger service commitment that has pushed patient satisfaction rates into the 90 percent range, from a starting point of around 50 percent. It's a fantastic example of the role that self-service can play in delivering service excellence.

And, yes, there are also operational advantages for Ochsner. Something about the self-scheduling process—perhaps it's a patient's heightened sense of agency and accountability or the ability to quickly view the full range of dates and times—has cut the no-show rate on appointments in half. In addition, the portal provides a new marketing platform to educate patients on the full range of the clinic's services. These advantages weren't free, of course. When the clinic realized that doctors and nurses had a big role in driving adoption, it doubled down on systems training. And it made the IT trainers responsible for *usage* as well as education, which meant they had a mandate to track down and support members of the clinic team who were slow to use the new system. Some doctors also resisted the sense that they were losing control of their own schedule. But the internal costs of the new technology were trumped by the improvement to the patient experience.

Now Ochsner has chosen not to charge its Baton Rouge patients extra for the new service, for a number of strategic reasons. But that's not the point. The point is that it *could*.

UNCOMMON TAKEAWAYS

✓ Service excellence must be funded in some way. If not, you risk delivering *gratuitous service,* service features that are donated to customers but never paid for in any way.

✓ There are four ways to fund a premium service experience: (1) get customers to pay you extra for it, (2) reduce costs in ways that also improve service, (3) improve service in ways that also reduce costs, or (4) get customers to enjoy doing some of the work for you.

✓ Method 1 is the simplest, at least from a design perspective. Methods 2 and 3 are the most reliable. Method 4 gets the most attention.

✓ Extra service fees aren't inherently good or bad. Their success depends on the specific contract you have with customers.

✓ A loyalty program is one way to get paid for a premium service experience. True loyalty programs— programs that increase customers' willingness to pay a premium price—are rare, largely because most loyalty programs are mislabeled retention programs.

✓ For self-service to be part of an uncommon service experience, customers must prefer self-service to a full-service alternative.

Chapter Three

Truth Number 3: It's Not Your Employees' Fault

When was the last time you had a frustrating interaction with a call center? Most of us can measure our answer in days. Here's what was probably happening on the other end of the line: the person you spoke to was watching as many as eight screens at once while trying to assist frustrated customers from all cultures, ages, and levels of expertise with a growing range of product and service needs. Given typical investments in salary and training, that person was either an effective communicator without the capacity to solve technical problems, or a competent technician with limited interpersonal skills. Neither one could reliably solve your problem.

The "bad guy" in this service failure, of course, isn't the overwhelmed and underskilled service rep. It's the system these employees were dropped into—a system that sets up employees to fail. If your company delivers disappointing service on a consistent basis, or even excellent service but only in fits and starts, it's not because you've somehow managed to hire an entire company of people who *just don't get it*. The problem is much more likely to be that you've built a service model for phantom employees you wish you had—but actually don't.

Try Harder, Fail Faster

Most companies aren't systematically delivering bad service. Most are inconsistent—sometimes they nail it; other times they miss. Episodic excellence is not good news. It's distracting. It's a shiny object that pulls you off your true target, even as it convinces you that everything's OK. And it often inspires what we call try-harder solutions.

A try-harder solution is built on the logic that if one employee can deliver excellence, then everyone else should be able to get there as well. Since one person can perform in the system (more likely, in spite of it), managers conclude that the input that matters most is individual effort. Our message is simple: it's not. The way you've designed the business—and specifically the employee management system—matters more.

First, not all of your employees are superheroes. Most companies have a continuum on the payroll, from the exceptionally talented to the should-definitely-be-doing-something-else-with-their-lives. This isn't easy to acknowledge. Any number of things can get in the way of doing so, from the role you played in hiring someone to good, old-fashioned conflict aversion. Here's a safe assumption: unless you have the resources and capacity to systematically attract, reward, and unleash the very best in your industry, some of the people now reporting to you cannot be objectively characterized as outstanding.

Second, you're probably making your employees' job harder. The hunt for new sources of revenue within organizations often leads to an increase in operational complexity. New products and services—or even new variations on old ones—lead to new processes, policies, and regulations; new organizational structures and technologies; new customers with new needs being channeled toward new touch points. In one quick-service restaurant we studied, the menu had grown from twenty-five items to more than a hundred in just a few years. Over that same period, the number of ways a cashier could ring up the restaurant's signature drink had grown to *fifty-five*. At another company—this one in telecom—the company's systems had become so complicated that it took thirteen months for the average employee to become proficient in them. Meanwhile, the average time that new employees stuck with the job was nine months. Customer satisfaction followed these employees out the door, bottoming out at 30 percent.

In short, the average employee is drowning in complexity. And the outstanding employee, the one who has a chance of keeping up, is a much scarcer resource than many managers are willing to acknowledge. We're designing jobs for superhumans, and it turns out our people are flesh and blood.

The Successful Employee Management System

In a service model that works, employees are reasonably able and reasonably motivated to achieve excellence. The *able* part is made possible by selection, training, and job designs that set up real-world employees to succeed. The *motivated* part is facilitated by a performance management system that makes them want to do their jobs effectively (and makes it hard to do them badly).

Bugs Burger Bug Killers (BBBK) (*Burger* has a soft g and rhymes with "merger") built an extraordinary service business by creating an employee management system that integrated and aligned four elements: selection, training, job design, and performance management.[1] Let's look at each of these elements.

Selection

At the height of its success, BBBK was the largest independent extermination company in America. With a growth rate north of 20 percent, the company served fifteen thousand clients in almost all fifty states. Its success was driven by its unique service offering and by the promise that lived at the heart of it. BBBK guaranteed complete pest *elimination,* as distinct from pest control, the business of its competitors. If the company failed to eliminate all pests in a reasonable amount of time, clients got a full refund plus a year's worth of another provider's service.

This was not what the rest of the industry was selling. No other company offered a performance guarantee with any bite. Instead, companies would commit to trying their best—often with poor results. But as the company's passionate founder, Al "Bugs" Burger, explained when describing why he started the business, "you reach a point where you rise out of . . . the mediocrity everybody allows themselves to be kept down by." In return for delivering excellence, BBBK's price premium was at least four to six times what the rest of the industry could charge. In some cases, that multiple drifted up to ten.

The company's competitive advantage? According to Burger, it was his people, specifically his frontline service specialists. Service specialists were treated like the organization's privileged class, and the hierarchy configured itself to set up these frontline workers to excel. One senior executive captured the company's mentality: "It's the service specialists that pay my salary."

Building an elite crew of service providers started with a rigorous selection process. The experience involved multiple rounds of interviews, not only with applicants, but also with their family members. There were lifestyle implications to becoming a mobile service provider who worked nights, and a supportive family network was critical to a specialist's success. Applicants were also subjected to rigorous personality and aptitude testing. Managers at the Miami headquarters ran the process, and only 2 to 3 percent of applicants made it to the final rounds. Final decisions were made by local service managers.

What were they looking for? BBBK recruited two specific employee profiles—perfectionists and potential managers who thrived on the idea of excellence. The process was designed entirely to identify these two types of individuals. Even the rigor of the experience helped attract the target profiles by reinforcing the message that BBBK was in a league of its own. And the balance of the two groups was as important as individual type. BBBK concluded that too many people with either profile threatened the culture and cohesion of its field teams.

Like BBBK, the real trick to selection is to know exactly which traits you're looking for—and then to design a process that reliably uncovers them. Southwest Airlines interviews potential hires in groups, bringing other employees and even customers into the process. In this setting of other job seekers, company representatives, and valued customers, an applicant is asked to stand up and describe his or her most embarrassing moment. Most people are shocked to hear that this playful airline has such an aggressive selection technique, assuming Southwest is playing hardball to test the speaker's confidence.

But it's not what it appears. When the person describing the most embarrassing moment is speaking, making himself or herself vulnerable to complete strangers who are competing for a job (yes, it's awkward), Southwest recruiters are watching the *other* applicants. Why? They're looking for clues to empathy, signals that an applicant feels bad for the storyteller. It turns out that empathy is the secret sauce to serving customers well at thirty thousand feet.

Should You Invest in the Best?

In an ideal world, all of your employees would be high in attitude and high in aptitude. These people inhabit the upper right quadrant of figure 3–1 (this is the same chart shown in figure 1–1). They are the highly motivated, dream-team employees who are also deliciously competent, the people you usually have in mind when mapping your route to uncommon service. The problem is, you're

FIGURE 3-1

The cost of hiring "stars": employees, who occupy the upper right quadrant of the chart, are expensive to recruit and retain

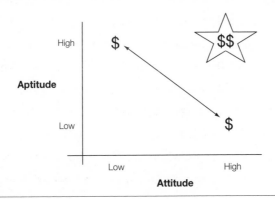

not the only one who wants these people, and as a result, they're expensive.

If you design a service model that requires the A-list employees of your industry, you must be able to pay for the privilege. Professional service firms like McKinsey & Company can afford to hire from the upper right quadrant of figure 3–1 because the firm receives a price premium from clients, which in turn permits McKinsey to invest heavily in attracting and retaining high achievers. For McKinsey, that investment includes high salaries and a disproportionate focus on professional development, including workshops held in exalted destinations such as the Austrian Alps.

Few companies can afford to make this kind of HR investment. The alternative is to design an employee management system that delivers outstanding results with lower-cost employees. As we detailed in chapter 1, Commerce Bank simplified each task in the overall service design, which allowed it to hire for enthusiasm but not financial skills.

How did Commerce handle selection? The bank literally needed fifteen seconds in an interview to know if someone would be a good fit. Within fifteen seconds, the Commerce interviewer could tell if prospective employees *smiled in a resting state.* Commerce Bank understood that most of us smile when provoked, but we spend most of our day with a more neutral or even negative expression on our face. A subset of human beings, however, smiles as a default position. Since an eight-hour day at Commerce required eight hours of smiling, the company looked for people with this "smiley gene."

Of course, first the bank had to get these happy people into the job interview. Commerce Bank decided to leverage its best asset for this task: a payroll already filled with happy people. Like any tribe, smilers are great at recognizing themselves in other people. And so Commerce distributed handfuls of laminated cards to new employees with a printed message inviting people to join the Commerce family. It then instructed new hires to hand out a card to anyone who gave them a great service experience. Literally anyone, Commerce told them— whether it was a great toll booth operator or librarian or convenience store cashier. With one exception—no one in the financial services industry, including another retail bank. The effort it took to deprogram these employees was too high, and they were likely to be too expensive, given the aptitude requirements of most banks and brokerages.

Training

New hires at BBBK spent five months in training. The industry standard at the time was no more than a few weeks for training, sometimes as little as a few days. As one manager remarked, BBBK's approach was "like boot camp in the army, only it's three times as long and twice as tough." The investment of time, energy, and money was a radical departure from the norm.

In these five months, new recruits were not treated like passive observers. Under the full-time instruction of a field manager, they were expected to learn quickly and reveal their ability to perform. Still, they were months away from being unleashed. Halfway into the training experience, recruits were sent to Miami for two weeks of intensive classroom learning. In month six, new service specialists finally got their own route. The total tab? It was $15,000 per specialist in the 1980s—about $30,000 in 2011 dollars.

The effort was focused as much on developing someone's technical ability as on exposing him—or her (BBBK didn't hesitate to hire women)—to the company's unique culture. The experience also reinforced the message, made clear in the selection process, that new hires were a vital part of the company's ability to succeed. The legendary "Bugs" himself made it a priority to participate actively in training, spending more than a day with each new class. He made it his job to motivate new employees and to embody the company's mission of service excellence.

This kind of cultural imprinting, which we'll explore more in chapter 5, is a hallmark of great service training. Quality control is another. At Commerce, new employees are brought together into a large room on their first day of orientation. The trainer at the front of the room begins by telling everyone, "You're all wack jobs!" The place is electric. Thirty seconds later, the facilitator tells everyone that at Commerce Bank, employees answer the phone with an attitude of "Wow!" He then instructs the new hires to pretend they have a phone in front of them, and on his count, everyone should answer the imaginary phone and say hello with an attitude of "Wow!" "One, two, three . . . Hello!"

An incredible thing happens next. A few recruits have had enough. They head for the exits, finally acting on a hunch they had from the beginning: this crazy place is not what they signed up for. The relentless friendliness is too much. Commerce Bank found a way to scare away these outliers on day one of training. As a result, the bank doesn't spend a penny on people who aren't deeply energized by being friendly to strangers, all day, every day, no matter what.

Zappos also tries to weed out misfits early in the investment, in part by channeling all new employees—from C-level hires to call center recruits—through the same four-week training program. This step reinforces one of the company's core values: "Be humble." Anyone who's uncomfortable with these values or the way they manifest in his or her job is encouraged to leave during the training stage. Strongly encouraged. Halfway through the training process, Zappos offers all new recruits $2,000 to walk away, no questions asked. The company has learned that anyone who values the fast cash over the long-term opportunity is not going to be a good hire.

Job Design

The alternative to rigorous training, of course, is a job design that is so intuitive that employees can do it on day one. Think of it as the anti-BBBK approach, a route to service excellence that is no less viable. It won't work in every industry, but the logic of it will: simplify the job so that your people can focus on service.

That's what LSQ Funding Group did when it built an innovative service model that allows small businesses to borrow quickly against their receivables. The industry—also known as *factoring*—has been around for centuries, but LSQ found a way to deliver unprecedented speed, transparency, and humanity. In most cases, clients get access to funds within hours, a transaction facilitated by passionate employees who turn over at a rate of less than 5 percent. This number is unheard-of in financial operations centers, which are often characterized as grim work environments that tend to churn through employees quickly.

By reducing the technical complexity of their jobs, LSQ virtually eliminated the need to train its employees. Rather than train new hires in the time-intensive operations and risk-management analytics specific to the factoring business, LSQ automated these processes with graceful, customized IT systems that can be operated with almost no previous experience. According to founder Max Eliscu, the technology enables new hires to immediately feel "capable and empowered." These dynamics allow the company not only to compete on things like speed and customer support, but also to prioritize attitude in the hiring process. Because of its IT platform, LSQ has the freedom to focus on identifying traits like cultural fit, service orientation, and attitude, the traits that distinguish the company in its client interactions.

Other companies have taken similar streamlined approaches to job design. Commerce Bank simplified its offering to match the profile of low-aptitude, high-attitude employees. Southwest also designed for simplicity, relying on only one type of airplane, the Boeing 737, and reducing the number of moving parts at every turn, including an industry-defying decision to refuse to transfer baggage to other airlines. Zappos made excellence an everyday occurrence, in part by designing the job of a call center employee so that a human being without the temperament and skills of an air traffic controller would not be overwhelmed. The folks answering phones at Zappos have only three screens to monitor. With the mechanics of the job under control, they're freed up to focus on exceeding the customer's expectations. By a long shot.

Again, the nemesis of good job design is complexity. Complexity has a bad habit of creeping into your systems and jobs over time, as you respond to dynamic market conditions and chase new sources of revenue. You may have tamed complexity five years ago with roles and responsibilities that matched your world of five years ago and your employees of five years ago. But the threat requires constant vigilance. What matters is whether your current job designs match the people who are doing them *right now*.

IT Solutions: Are You Hurting or Helping Your People?

IT tools that work are deeply thoughtful about the user experience, including how and when data is entered in the rhythm of a particular job. Ideally, they're developed in tandem with the role itself. This rarely happens. Typically, a job is designed, technology advances, and then the technology is piled on as an afterthought. The result—predictably—is an increased operational burden on employees and its familiar by-product: widespread resentment. In an excellent, ongoing discussion presented in his blog, Andrew McAfee of MIT discusses how to mitigate this risk and integrate IT productively into your organization.[a]

An IT solution that's easy to use tends to mean a very sophisticated system running under the hood. And it's rarely cheap to build and maintain. Off-the-shelf solutions such as software by Salesforce.com can be excellent, affordable alternatives, but if you need something more customized, be prepared to fund it. For example, LSQ spends about 7 percent of revenues on IT, compared with less than 1 percent industry-wide. But the investment can be worth it, particularly if it pays off in other ways, too. In LSQ's case, the advantage of its IT systems goes well beyond a job design that allows its people to truly be of service. LSQ's systems provide a platform for organizational speed and transparency, the keys to the company's positioning. The model also allows for greater upward mobility among employees. People are less specialized, and few walk around with precious institutional knowledge that isn't captured intuitively on the company's servers. This means that because no one is structurally locked into a job, each person has the freedom to move quickly to the next level of challenge and growth. It also means that almost any staff member can quickly and conclusively address a client's request. Perhaps most important, it makes the service model highly scalable, which is why LSQ is now poised to grow faster than any other player in the industry.

Unfortunately, this is often not how the IT story plays out in service industries. Too often, well-intentioned systems end up hurting productivity rather than helping it. At one health-care company we studied, patient information was very thoughtfully digitized, but there were not enough computer terminals to accommodate the full team of physicians, including visiting doctors, who were an important part of the delivery model. Moreover, doctors had to log into individual computers each time they wanted to use the system, but if they did not fully log out after a session, they would have to go back to the specific terminal they had been working on and completely log out before getting access to the system again. A busy physician making rounds might see six patients on six different floors or wings that all looked very much alike. But the doctor would literally have to go hunting through the hospital for the one terminal where he or she hadn't properly exited, a frequent exercise in organizational fury. This was not a marriage of technology and job design leading to better patient care.

Here's the basic message: be prepared to go all the way in integrating technology into job design, from great software and functional hardware to effective training and regular user feedback. Stopping short can be a disaster. And the value of reaching the finish line may surprise you.

a. Andrew McAfee, "Andrew McAfee's Blog: The Business Impact of IT," http://andrewmcafee.org/blog.

Performance Management

Job design is mostly about designing tasks so that they match a typical employee's attitude and aptitude. Performance management is about creating incentives to do a job well—and disincentives to do it poorly. These are the carrots and sticks that keep your employees on track, but they can also include controls such as scripts and checklists that make it difficult for employees to stray too far.[2]

BBBK employees had access to many carrots that sound familiar, but were novel for the industry: good salaries, a 20 percent cut of billings on their routes, profit sharing, performance bonuses. These things made a difference, promoting a sense of ownership among employees and signaling that BBBK was not doing business as usual. But the incentives worked because they were combined with another departure from performance norms. The company demanded total access to information.

Specialists had lots of autonomy—they worked unsupervised and set their own schedules. Many reported that managing a route felt like owning your own business. At the end of each monthly service call, however, a specialist was required to cough up every detail about the client interaction. Literally everything, from the customer's sanitation habits to the slightest evidence that a bug might have checked the place out. Employees were also asked to declare, in writing, whether they needed any help on the account. And help was more than readily available, even if it meant flying in out-of-state specialists when a site suddenly needed urgent attention. From early in the hiring process, the message was clear: mistakes were forgiven; liars were not.

A few days after a specialist's visit, a client got a call from a district manager, who followed up on the specialist's monthly report. The specialist performed the work, but his or her manager circled back to the customer. This division of labor created a powerful incentive to deliver excellence, as feedback on the specialist's work was solicited immediately. And it made misrepresenting the truth (e.g., blaming the client for any problems) distinctly unappealing. In addition, a full-time quality control team traveled around the country visiting customers and filing its own reports. Specialists didn't know if or when this team would be showing up on their routes. As one route man said, "It's pressure, but it helps you keep up your standards. Without it, I guess we'd be just like any other company." Another agreed: "It gives us that little extra motivation."

It also allowed the company to protect the specialist from noncompliant customers. If customers didn't follow the cleanup regimen the specialist designed, they were dropped as clients, and the employee was subsidized until another customer was found to fill out the route. We'll spend more time on the issue of customer management and BBBK's approach in chapter 4. Suffice it to say that your management role doesn't end with your employees.

BBBK's performance management tools worked for BBBK. They helped the company deliver outstanding service in an industry marked by indifference, if not downright fraud. One of the company's clients was so moved by what he observed that he quit his job as a restaurant manager on the spot and vowed to help build the business: "It was the middle of the night, and here were these five guys, filthy dirty, crawling under and into everything, just doing a super job . . . After a while one guy got up off the floor . . . I didn't know it at first, but he was the boss . . . anybody who can motivate people to do this kind of work, I want to be associated with him."

Scenes like this played out across the country. And they did because BBBK's incentives to excel not only worked for individuals, but they also worked seamlessly with the rest of its employee management system.

We're not suggesting that the company's approach is somehow universal, although its deliberate balance of "trust and verify" shows up in the management systems of many other successful service companies. Rather, our central point here is to trust your instincts and get creative. That's what "Bugs" did to get results, even as his peers in the industry initially dismissed his practices as crazy. Customize your strategy to the unique needs and opportunities of your own company. Resist relying exclusively on standard performance levers, no matter how entrenched they are in your industry.

Who Gets a Script?

We tend to associate scripts with lower-wage employees, call-center operators without enough training or breathing room to improvise answers for a flood of angry customers. But Canadian retailer Spence Diamonds has revealed the power of writing dialogue for even $100,000-plus employees. Spence built a high-growth retail jewelry business with margins that are double the industry average. Counterintuitively, Spence gets there by delivering outstanding service through the highest-paid salespeople in the business. Even less intuitively, its success is driven by a highly scripted sales process that tells veteran salespeople exactly what to say, when to say it, where to stand—even where to put their pens throughout a conversation.

Spence pays its experienced "diamond consultants" more than twice the industry standard. CEO Sean Jones describes managing these salespeople as being "like managing an NBA team," with all the sensitivity toward egos, team chemistry, and playing time. Everyone is an individual performer, and everyone is at the top of his or her game. And Jones's job is to get his squad members to do something truly bizarre: don't trust their instincts, even when those instincts allowed them to dominate every other sales environment. Learn the script. All seventy pages of it. And stick to it, even when they feel confident enough to start tweaking the process.

Why the rigid process? Jones discovered that his salespeople were *six times* more likely to be effective if they followed "the Spence way," step by tiny step, from the moment a customer walked into the store to the moment he or she signed on the dotted line. The entire process is designed, with scientific precision, to find out exactly what customers want and to help them feel confident acting on it. Founder Doug Spence's core insight, which Jones ran with, was that the typical engagement-ring buyer (young, male) is terrified when he walks in the door. Not just a little bit anxious or intimidated. Terrified. And not just of the product, but of the institution it represents. Marriage is heady stuff. Piled onto that base level of fear is often the sickening awareness that he will be judged by friends and family on whatever ring he selects. This is quickly followed by another unsettling thought, often the moment the customer crosses the threshold of a jewelry store: he knows nothing about diamonds. Cut, color, clarity, carats. It's an obscure new language, and he doesn't speak a word of it.

Many jewelers do little to reduce the engagement ring buyer's anxiety. The client steps into a hushed, feminine domain. A small selection of merchandise is typically locked up under thick glass cabinets. A conspicuously armed guard is on patrol, reinforcing the buyer's sneaking suspicion that he's in the wrong place at the wrong time. With consequences. Contrast that experience with "the Spence way": a friendly and accessible atmosphere, open cabinets filled with thousands of prototypes made of cubic zirconia that the client can touch and feel, a personalized education on the basics of diamond grading. And the Spence customer gets to interact with a friendly consultant, who knows exactly the right words to say, at exactly the right time, to help the buyer make the decision of a lifetime.

The scripts aren't the only reason the model works. Like other successful service businesses, Spence Diamonds has decided where to excel (selection, service, price) and where to underperform (location, brand). It only invests in one location per market and finds retail space that is near a premium location, but outside the real estate sweet spots, where prices are significantly higher. The company has also figured out how to deliver excellence with *fewer, better* people, a model that's underutilized in many service industries. Spence pays its people significantly more, but it doesn't need as many of them.

And yet Jones maintains that the company's real competitive advantage is its sales script. Spence is now the most profitable jeweler in Canada and is looking toward global expansion. Its biggest barrier to growth? Finding great players to move diamonds with empathy on the retail floor—and finding great coaches who can keep them on script.

Evidence is mounting that many of our most familiar tools aren't actually effective at motivating employee behavior. There's some fantastic research going on now to challenge the conventional wisdom on even the most basic of incentives. Consider tipping. Michael Lynn, professor of consumer behavior and marketing at Cornell University, argues there's a correlation of less than 11 percent between the quality of the service and the size of the tip.[3] Famed restaurateur Alice Waters highlighted another problem: even assuming that the prospect of a good tip motivates the serving staff, tipping does nothing to motivate the kitchen staff. As Waters pointed out when she dispensed with discretionary tipping and instituted a 17 percent service charge at her legendary Chez Panisse, an attentive waiter won't be able to fill the reservation book if the food itself is mediocre.

Sometimes the answer is more than one system within the same organizational umbrella, designed around different people and functions. Most sales-oriented organizations already do some form of this, paying the sales force for performance, while putting others on salary. But customization can also mean thinking creatively about status-based rewards. See what happens to the IT team's motivation when you take its offices out of the basement.

And sometimes, performance management needs to be an entirely homegrown phenomenon. When Commerce employees see each other doing well, they give out stickers saying "Great Job" or "Keep Going." This system may not work well for brokers at Citigroup, but it provides normative incentives that match the team environment and "people people" at Commerce.

Performance management at Brazilian retail giant Magazine Luiza includes Monday morning pep rallies that start at 7:45 a.m. It's consistent with the rest of the company's employee management system, which is focused sharply on upward mobility, an incentive program it calls Assisted Freedom. The program dictates that if you want the manager's job, you must articulate how you will help the manager get the promotion that will clear the way for you to advance.

Magazine Luiza continues to defy conventional performance management wisdom by maintaining a huge database on the behavior of its customers—many of them poor and rural—including individual buying cycles. When things get slow on the floor, cashiers are encouraged to contact customers who appear inactive. Thirty-five percent of compensation for everyone, including these cashiers, is variable pay based on sales.

And like everything else, performance management should be dynamic, responsive to both internal and external changes. Tipping once worked for Celebrity Cruises, but Celebrity customers increasingly started coming from outside North America. Tipping is far less of a norm in Europe, and it is frowned upon in parts of Asia. Whereas the company once had to provide no more than 10 percent of its employees' compensation, counting on customers to help motivate crew members, it recently had to revamp its compensation policy.

Finally, keep in mind that money may not be the most powerful incentive for your employees. Research keeps piling up that recognition and status may matter even more, along with a sense of purpose and belonging. Everyone needs to believe that what he or she does matters. The implications of these findings are not easy to digest, particularly in industries where compensation models seem too established to tweak. But companies that get it are seeing results. The Cleveland Clinic, which consistently ranks as one of the best hospitals in the world, is a pioneering center for cardiac and diabetes care. Its physicians are not paid on a fee-for-service basis, the typical health-care model, but are instead salaried employees. Apparently, what motivates them to provide such extraordinary service is something inherent in the work itself and in the privilege of being part of an exceptional team.

Our central point here, as elsewhere, is that your performance management system has to be both internally consistent and integrated well into the rest of your business model. All the parts have to work together.

CASE STUDY
Innovating at Verizon Call Centers

Verizon wrestled with the importance of an integrated employee management system when it was staffing up call centers to service two separate business lines—its traditional local and long distance business and its new DSL offering. Local and long distance worked beautifully along the four elements of an employee management system: Verizon knew just whom to select (people who like building up expertise with repetitive tasks) and just how to train them. These new hires received three months of intensive training that set them up to execute seamlessly on a job design that was very well understood. And performance management was relatively easy with phone scripts that gave employees very little latitude on what they could say to customers, who were highly unlikely to be calling in with something the company hadn't heard before.

It all fell apart next door at the DSL call center, at least initially. Because it was difficult to anticipate what DSL customers were going to say when they called, scripts weren't particularly helpful. People who liked repetitive tasks were likely to get anxious and flustered with the uncertainty of customer demands, and so the company needed to hire an entirely new type of employee, the type that was comfortable with ambiguity and excited by variation. Verizon needed to hire new people who could help them to *learn*—a critical distinction in organizational goals that our colleague Amy Edmondson has articulated.[a] And there was no use putting these hires through a three-month training program when the company did not yet know what the job would actually entail. Ultimately, Verizon built a successful new employee management system for its emerging DSL business, but not before trying to import the old one. After more than a few rock-star local and long distance employees crashed and burned in the instability of the DSL universe, the company went back to the drawing board.

a. Amy C. Edmondson, *Teaming: How Organizations Learn, Innovate, and Compete* (San Francisco: Jossey-Bass, 2012).

Putting It into Practice

If the service you're delivering is disappointing—if it's average or spotty in a model you assumed would produce reliable excellence—a common explanation is a mismatch between your employees and the jobs you've tasked them to do. Sound at all familiar? If so, we advise companies to first try to get a sense of the size of the employee-job gap. We suggest two diagnostic steps that will produce some intuition about the magnitude of the problem. If you have a few days to study the question, start with the approach described below. If you only have a few minutes, skip to the second step.

1. Go Undercover (Estimated Time: One or Two Days)

Get out of the politicized back office, and go see what's happening on the front lines of your organization. If you need inspiration, watch a few episodes of CBS's *Undercover Boss,* which follows senior executives of large organizations as they slip into the trenches. It's actually good television: a dramatic arc, the conquering of obstacles (the jobs the CEOs take on are often a lot harder than they expect), the discovery of light and truth on the other side (episodes often end with humbled, wide-eyed executives vowing to change the employee experience). As a viewer, you also have no choice but to reflect on your own distorted assumptions about the experience of the people around you. You can't help but identify with the protagonists as they stumble past the fun-house mirrors of their own minds. Anyway, consider the show emotional fuel for your own fact-finding journey.

A hidden identity isn't easy to pull off in most companies, but the next best thing is almost as effective: talk frankly with your people about their experience on the job, what makes it easy or hard, and how their roles have changed over time. Watch them in action. Try to do an average employee's job for a day, and see how you fare. Take a seat at your call center, and try to respond to eight screens of information at once.

We recommend spending the equivalent of at least two days on this exercise, gathering data from a range of perspectives. Most executives will discover some level of mismatch between employees and jobs, and will be able to determine whether it's a serious threat to the service experience.

2. Chart Complexity over Time (Estimated Time: Fifteen Minutes)

Once you have some intuition from going undercover, try to graphically plot how the operational complexity experienced by your employees has changed over the past five years (this can be done for any job). Then plot the change in employee sophistication over the same time span. If your graph looks something like figure 3–2, then you have a problem.

FIGURE 3-2

The competence-complexity gap

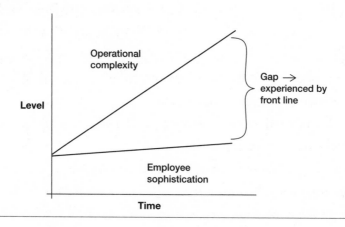

Some groups we've worked with skip the first step and just do this simple chart exercise. Sometimes that's enough to surface the issue. It often leads to thoughtful conversations about the true costs of the gap—an increasingly painful service experience, an overwhelmed workforce. These costs tend to be absorbed by customers and by the least empowered people on the payroll, the ones least likely to complain about it. These are the stakeholders carrying the burden of the mismatch, and it's management's job to relieve them.

3. Close the Gap

When a company identifies a gap between its people and the jobs they're doing, it essentially has two choices: reduce operational complexity or increase employee sophistication. Said differently, change the people or change the job. On the people side, the two levers you have are selection and training. Selection might work in a high-turnover business, but it's usually a daunting solution for any other organization. Most organizations don't have the time, ruthlessness, or resources to swap out their employees. Training is an option, but there's a risk of underestimating—often dramatically—how much of it is required. Overcoming a large skill gap requires a substantial amount of investment and management attention. A two-day training seminar won't turn a flight attendant into a pilot.

So what do you do?

The goal is to get a closer match between employee sophistication and operational complexity. Go as far as you can on the people front, and then address system complexity. You can address complexity either by decreasing it outright or by decreasing the amount of complexity experienced by each employee.

For the latter, it may be possible to more thoughtfully break up who does what—break down a job into smaller tasks and assign them to specialized employees. Take inspiration from a hospital: one person takes blood pressure, another does anesthesia, and another performs the surgery. The system itself is complicated, but each employee only experiences a portion of it.

There's a certain amount of hand-off risk for customers in models like these, where specialists pass customers along to other specialists. If you choose this route, there is an increased need for systems that facilitate exquisite communication across people and tasks. IT has a role to play here by capturing information in a centralized location that everyone on the team can access. LSQ Funding Group used this approach, with dramatic results. Similarly, a concierge-type customer advocate— increasingly common in health care—can help clients navigate the complexity of a large service organization.

Ready to take on system-wide complexity? We suggest starting with back-end complexity that's adding little to the customer experience. Reduce those fifty-five ways your employees can ring up the same drink, since numbers 2 through 55 do nothing to make the drink experience more enjoyable. This is the type of operational confusion that we classify as a high-complexity, low-value-added operation (figure 3–3).

Once you've cleaned up this type of chaos, you can take on the complexity that's actually improving the customer experience. This is a much harder change, as internal buy-in can be harder to achieve, and some ingenuity is needed to buffer customers from the change. The goal is to move down to the lower-right hand side of the chart in figure 3–3. How can you reduce complexity without undermining service levels?

FIGURE 3-3

Where to start attacking system-wide complexity

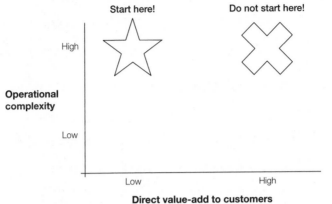

At one quick-serve restaurant we studied, the exploding number of items on the menu was becoming a barrier to the employees' ability to deliver consistent, effective service—in addition to driving up costs and confusing the marketing message. When this company's franchisees gathered for their annual meeting, everyone agreed that menu rationalization was a top priority. Heads nodded all around the room. But when the group got down to the task of actually simplifying the menu, no one could agree on removing a *single* item from the list. Every dessert, every bargain meal, found a passionate defender. It represented revenue to someone, somewhere. Meanwhile, the collective list was driving performance into the ground.

How to move forward? This company acknowledged the inability to get there by consensus and nominated a steering committee of trusted members to make thoughtful decisions on its behalf. Most important, it didn't walk away from the challenge. However you choose to make progress, you must *act.* Operational complexity is a real challenge at most organizations, more so at organizations with their eyes on the service-excellence prize. It's the type of challenge that's often difficult to see when you're in the middle of it, even as it's crippling your ability to excel.

UNCOMMON TAKEAWAYS

✓ The goal of an excellent service organization is to deliver outstanding results with average employees.

✓ Many companies design service models for employees they don't have—for a payroll filled with superstars when, in fact, there's a healthy range of talent and initiative on the team. Capture this reality in the design of the business model.

✓ Successful employee management systems have four main components: selection, training, job design, and performance management. These components must be internally consistent and aligned with the rest of the service model. There's no such thing as good or bad selection, for example. The issue is whether it's consistent with the rest of the employee management system and whether the system is consistent with the rest of the service model.

✓ IT solutions can help or hurt your employees' productivity, often in dramatic ways. IT tools that work are sensitive to the employee experience, including how and when data is entered in the rhythm of a particular job. The best solutions are developed in tandem with the role itself—not piled on after a job design is already in place.

✓ The average service employee is overwhelmed by the increasing complexity of his or her job. When a company identifies a gap like this between operational complexity and employee sophistication, it has two choices: change the people or change the job. In other words, (1) train and hire differently or (2) redesign the job so that your current team can do it.

Chapter Four

Truth Number 4:
You Must Manage
Your Customers

Customers who can't decide what to order at McDonald's make the fast food less fast for everyone behind them. Airline passengers threaten on-time arrivals when they block the aisles while boarding. If a consulting firm's clients describe their needs in vague terms, they undermine the value of the advice they get. Even if it's just by showing up late for a dinner reservation (or by lingering over the espresso), restaurant patrons regularly disrupt their experience and the experience of other diners.

We've spent a lot of time thinking about the special role that customers often play in service encounters, a phenomenon we call the *customer-operator*. When it takes a customer five minutes to supersize an order of fries, he or she isn't just a passive recipient of your company's ingenuity and hard work. This person is now playing an active role in the delivery of the experience. Said differently, customers don't just consume service; they also participate in *creating* it. And they're not always good at their job.

Customers can increase the cost and reduce the quality of whatever service you're providing, often with no advance warning and very little regret. Sometimes they can help on both fronts (more on that later), but that's the exception, not the norm. Given these dynamics, a fair question is why they get any operating role at all. After all, Sony doesn't let its customers help to manufacture the television they're buying. The answer, in most cases, is that you have no choice. You chose to work in a service industry. You can't cut hair without a customer plopping down in front of you, and you can't teach a course without students who are willing to come to class. So how do you get your customer-operators to behave?

Customers (aka Your Unpaid, Untrained, Unmotivated Employees)

Here's one way to think about it: if you run a service business, then your customers "work" for you in many of the same ways that your employees do. But these aren't your average employees. They're erratic, unskilled, and entitled. Their interests and your interests regularly diverge. Employees are contractually bound to work on behalf of the firm, but customers operate under no such constraints. Customers are looking out for number one, as they have every right to do.

On the plus side, of course, customer-operators require no salary, benefits, or retirement contributions, and they show up precisely at the time service is required. They also have a level of insight into their individual tastes and quirks—insight that your employees won't ever have, even after throwing a fortune at market research. These factors suggest that there's a lot to be gained by empowering customers to play a greater role in meeting their own service needs.

Until recently, many executives saw a clear distinction between the people who produce goods and services, and the people who consume them—between the employees on the payroll and answerable to management, and the customers who exist somewhere outside the company's boundaries and its direct control. These days, a growing number of firms are expanding the productive role of customers to reduce costs or improve service, or both, with the proliferation of self-service as the most visible example.

But to manage customers in an operating role, a firm needs new strategies, since it can't rely on the same systems it uses for employees. Customers aren't dependent on the company for their livelihoods. They haven't signed a W-2 form and agreed to abide by certain rules and expectations in exchange for a weekly paycheck. As a result, powerful employee performance incentives such as career advancement and financial security are missing from the customer management tool kit. There's also rarely a rigorous selection or training process, at least not one focused on operational fit, and so you often have to work with whoever shows up, regardless of skill level or attitude. Oh, and there's typically a lot more of them. Customers outnumber employees by orders of magnitude in most companies.

To complicate matters further, not only are customers categorically different from employees, but customers can also be dramatically different from each other. This diversity dramatically increases the variability that is introduced onto the "factory floor" of service production. Variability of operating inputs (materials, processing time, worker skill) is public enemy number one in a manufacturing environment. It's the barrier to the critical goal of 100 percent utilization. But service managers are constantly being inundated with variability, in the form of customer-operators who are *a little bit different* from the last one who showed up—a little faster, slower, smarter, pickier, later, earlier, or more or less prepared to do the job. And every once in a while, through door number 2, comes a customer-operator who's a whole lot different. It's enough to make you crazy—and certainly enough to shrink your margins and ensure a mediocre service experience.

Here's the basic message: if you're in the service business, you essentially don't know which people are on your team, when they're showing up, and what they're going to do once they get there. And so you need a plan for managing this uncertainty.

Managing the Chaos of Customers

In other words, variability is a fact of life with customer-operators. Here are the different forms it can take:

- *Arrival:* Your customers don't all want service at the same time or at times that are necessarily convenient for you. Grocery stores find themselves swamped during the evening rush hour, while the lines at Dunkin' Donuts can extend for half a block at 8:00 a.m.

- *Request:* Not everybody orders the same thing. Each client of an advertising agency is executing a unique marketing strategy, and vacationers at a resort want different amenities. Even customers of a single-service business like Jiffy Lube show up in different makes and models of cars.

- *Capability:* Customers have different knowledge, skill, physical abilities, and resources, which means that some customers perform tasks easily while others need hand-holding. In a medical setting, the ability of a patient to describe symptoms can greatly affect the quality of care. But so can the person's ability to negotiate the medical bureaucracy.

- *Effort:* Customer-operators decide for themselves how much effort to invest in production tasks. Company controllers don't always hand over well-organized files to independent auditors, and shoppers don't always return their shopping carts to the store.

- *Preference:* Even customers who want the same service may have very different definitions of quality. One diner appreciates the servers' introducing themselves by name; another resents the presumption of intimacy. Some clients of a law firm might construe a top partner's attention to detail as reflecting the importance of their case; others might complain that those expensive billable hours could be doled out more judiciously to less costly associates. Subjective preference adds a multiplier effect to all other forms of customer variability.

Knowing which type of variability you're dealing with can help you to manage it more effectively. Managing effort variability (often through incentives), for example, can differ markedly from managing capability variability (often through customer training initiatives).

You can manage customer chaos in essentially two ways: by reducing or accommodating it (figure 4–1). Reduction tends to favor efficiency. Accommodation tends to favor service, which keeps the two approaches in constant tension. Classic reduction strategies are menus and reservations. Limit your customers' options—a win for you, but a loss for your customers, who may be craving something off-menu that night and at some time other than 7:30 p.m. Accommodation, otherwise known as dealing, usually involves putting slack into the system and retaining a bench of experienced employees who can skillfully adapt to the chaos that customers bring with

FIGURE 4-1

Overcoming the trade-off between efficiency and service

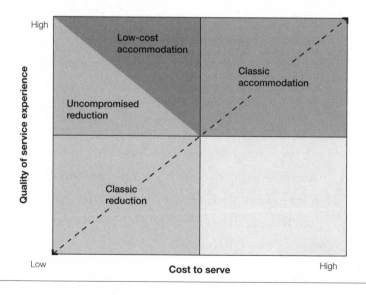

them. This approach is expensive. As a result, accommodation often hinges on getting customers to pay a premium, not always an option for your business.

But customer variability doesn't always force you into a stark trade-off between cost and quality. Self-service is the low-cost accommodation of choice in managing arrival and request variability. Self-service asks customers to deal with their own preferences on their own time line. It allows you to forgo complicated, inefficient labor scheduling and the deep (and expensive) bench of employees. When customers are doing the work, the right amount of labor is provided at exactly the right moment to deliver exactly the right kind of service.

Asking customers to roll up their sleeves isn't the only way around the tension between cost and accommodation. When Dell Computer Corporation first expanded into high-end servers, the company knew the corporate market for these machines would create significant new service demands, which it would have to accommodate with around-the-clock assistance. Dell faced a choice between destroying its margins by creating an underutilized and expensive service infrastructure or falling behind competitors that had more-efficient operations. Dell landed on a creative solution—outsourcing service to a third-party provider optimized for these kinds of twenty-four-hour, on-site service calls. By doing so, Dell reduced its exposure to customer variability by essentially handing off the challenge to a company better prepared to manage the challenge. The move created a buffer. Interestingly, Dell made a bold decision to outsource the servicing of its customers to its *competition*. Why? Because the strategy allowed Dell to deliver excellence without being overwhelmed by variability—and this advantage outweighed the risks of customer poaching.

There are more aspects of the variability question, but our point here is fairly simple: customers can wreak havoc on your operations. It's what makes us hesitate when we hear "the customer is always right" or that the path to service excellence is to simply delight your clients. Performance can't be sustained by placing customers on a pedestal and indulging their every desire.[1] To create a system in which excellence is the norm, you need to manage your customers every bit as much as you manage your employees.

Unleashing Customers at Shouldice Hospital

In the 1980s, HBS colleague Jim Heskett did a classic study of Shouldice Hospital, a Canadian institution focused on hernia surgery, which built a masterful business model in close collaboration with its customers—the patients it serves.[2] The extraordinary care that Shouldice provides is evidenced not only by statistical outcomes, but also by the loyalty of its clients. The Shouldice experience is so positive that many patients ask to stay an extra day. The most common "complication" of a surgical procedure is a mild sunburn acquired while a patient strolls the hospital's lawn.

Seeds of the Shouldice model were planted in 1932, when surgeon Earle Shouldice performed an appendectomy on a seven-year-old girl who refused to stay quietly in bed during the recovery period. Despite her incessant activity, the young girl recovered right on schedule. When Shouldice performed hernia repairs on four men a few years later, he allowed them to get out of bed right at the outset of their recovery. They, too, bounced back quickly, which solidified his belief that getting patients up and about, also known as *early ambulation*, could be an important part of the healing process. The catch, of course, was getting patients to do their part.

Shouldice used these experiences to develop a new methodology for treating hernia patients. It integrated early ambulation with an innovative surgical technique, a customized facility, and a very specific recovery regimen. The protocol relied heavily on teamwork and paid particular attention to patient selection. The hernia sufferers that Shouldice agreed to treat were limited to those who could participate fully and thereby benefit fully. This meant that they had to be otherwise healthy, not overweight, and willing to embrace the get-up-and-go concept.

Shouldice's unique approach was eventually institutionalized. Today, Shouldice Hospital starts managing its customers right from the beginning. The hospital sends out a confirmation card that explains the selection requirements—including weight limits—as well as the hospital's distinctive protocols. For those who are only moderately overweight at the time of scheduling, Shouldice outlines a weight-loss program. If weight guidelines are not met by the date scheduled for hospital admission, the patient is rejected.

Once a Shouldice customer is cleared to proceed, the person's job has only just begun. Each afternoon, on the day before they're scheduled for surgery, about thirty new patients arrive at the clinic. While receiving preliminary tests, they are expected to meet and mingle with the other members of their incoming "class." At this point, patients begin to realize they are not passive recipients of care, but active members of a special Shouldice community in which they have many important roles to play.

At 5 p.m., nurses provide a formal orientation with information about what to expect, the drugs to be administered, the need for exercise after the operation, and the early-ambulatory recovery routine. Patients then eat dinner together in a hundred-seat dining room. This is followed at 9 p.m. by a kind of freshman mixer, where preoperative patients mingle with patients who completed their procedures earlier that day. Here, a tremendous amount of learning passes from the post-op "trainers" to the pre-op newbies, with no employees in sight, except for a few roaming waitstaff carrying platters of cookies. After this orientation and swapping of stories, it's time for bed.

The next morning, during the procedure itself, patients are usually fully alert and able to converse with their surgeon. Then, when the incision is closed, the surgeon extends a helpful arm and invites the patient to get off the operating table and walk to the recovery room. Ninety-nine percent of patients take this postsurgical stroll, which aside from promoting the body's circulation, delivers a strong psychic jolt to the healing process.

From that moment on, patients are encouraged by nurses and housekeepers to continue their gentle exercise. There are no bedpans at Shouldice, no telephones or television sets in the rooms. Patients are expected to be out and about, walking the twenty acres of grounds, playing shuffleboard or pool, negotiating custom-designed stairs, and mingling with the other patients. At 9 p.m. on the day of their surgery, they walk down to the dining room for the tea and cookies orientation for incoming patients. On the fourth morning, they are ready for discharge. Many don't want to leave.

Sixty years after its launch, Shouldice Hospital performs roughly 7,500 hernia operations a year. For the more than 300,000 procedures the hospital has performed, the rate of recurrence is 1 percent, compared with 6 percent in hospitals relying on more traditional methods.

Shouldice is a special place. The hospital achieves these extraordinary results by getting patients to play a highly active role not just in the delivery of their own health care, but also in the delivery of other patients' care. To get there, Shouldice Hospital focuses on many of the same core elements we highlighted in our discussion of employee management systems: selection, training, job design, and performance management. But this time, it's all about the customers.

The Successful Customer Management System

In designing a customer management system, we propose many of the same strategies that we used for employee management.

Customer Selection

By narrowing its focus on a particular procedure for a particular kind of patient, Shouldice Hospital achieves a highly predictable work environment with just the kind of low-risk, high-reward "customer" that every surgeon dreams of. The system wouldn't work if the hospital's doors were open to all.

In a world where no one is turned away, Shouldice couldn't operate at the same level of precision. For example, healthy men typically require the same length of incision and the same time for a procedure. Vary the types of customers coming in, and you vary the operating environment in ways that compound on each other. One patient takes a little longer, the schedule needs to accommodate the delay, and the next patients run late. Soon some doctors are staying late and some folks are missing orientation. An open door approach would also prevent the hospital from making significant demands on its patients.

In this way, Shouldice is less like a company hustling for customers and more like an elite university, with admissions policies that select only a very narrow band of highly skilled students. For these schools, in addition to the prestige of being discriminating and the increased likelihood that they will advance the state of our collective knowledge, it's also far more efficient to focus on a subset of students that's very aligned with their offerings. A wide range of student skill levels—a key driver of variability—is part of what makes large-scale public education so difficult and expensive. Stanford University and MIT don't have to devote resources to remedial learning.

For most companies, screening customers usually means checking their credit, not evaluating their fit from an operational perspective. But that is precisely what many service companies should be doing. Progressive Insurance is just as selective as Shouldice (or Stanford University or MIT) in choosing the customers it wants to do business with. Recall its comparison quote service from chapter 2. When Progressive delivers a quote on an auto policy, its price is the lowest only about half the time. In this model, the customers that the company doesn't want—the cost-sensitive ones who are also likely to misbehave on the road—go to the lower-priced competitor. And the good ones stick around. Of course, Progressive dresses up this customer selection strategy in the form of a value-added service. Save time by getting all your quotes in one place!

Think of all the resources you devote to hiring good employees: interviews; background checks; references; tests for ability, motivation, and cultural fit. Now think of the energy you spend on "hiring" the right customers. In most companies, there's no comparison, even though customer behavior can have just as much of an operational impact as employee behavior. Customers can play a defining role in your ability to deliver great service at a sustainable cost. And the greater your expectations for your customer-operators, the more time you need to devote to choosing the right people for the job.

Customer Training

Even the right customers often need training to perform their roles effectively. Sometimes this is part of the value proposition. The client of a yoga studio seeks proficiency in the poses, which allows the person to participate at a higher level and get dramatically more out of the experience. The same was true at Shouldice, where patients were eager to learn what they could do to speed up their recovery and stay healthy after discharge.

But training often needs to be dressed up a bit to make the concept palatable to customers. At Starbucks, customers have little awareness of being trained, even though it's a central part of the Starbucks service model.

Are you someone who resents having to say "tall" when ordering a small cup of coffee? Starbucks appreciates you playing along. The iconic coffee chain discovered long ago that customers who went with their gut while ordering ("Could you use skim milk instead of whole milk, and make sure it's hot and use that cup over there . . . no, the *other* small one . . . ") confused the baristas and destroyed the speed of service.

The solution was to train customers in a new shorthand for ordering Starbucks drinks. Training begins with a helpful booklet, which customers can take home and study on their own time. Here we learn all about "tall" and "venti," as well as the best way to order the different elements of a drink. Most important, we learn that it's OK if we get it wrong—our friends on the other side of the counter will be there to help us out, every step of the way (figure 4–2).

The booklet serves another purpose as well, which is to tee up the heart of the Starbucks customer training strategy: a program of subliminal influence that involves repeating orders back in Starbucks-speak. A customer who orders a small latte with two shots of espresso and skim milk instead of whole milk gets her order repeated back as a "double tall nonfat latte." Hold the extra words.

The protocol teaches customers the *right* way to do it, and everyone else in line overhears the tutorial. Most important, everyone else in line overhears if the customer gets it wrong, which is a powerful incentive for most human beings to scramble their way up the Starbucks-speak learning curve. And the proud few who refuse to do so (you know who you are) get their own little surge of satisfaction from quietly defying the Corporate Man. Everybody wins.

FIGURE 4-2

Customer training at Starbucks

HOW TO ORDER

If you're nervous about ordering, don't be.

There's no "right" way to order at Starbucks. Just tell us what you want and we'll get it to you. But if we call your drink back in a way that's different from what you told us, we're not correcting you. We're just translating your order into "barista-speak"—a standard way our baristas call out orders. This language gives the baristas the info they need in the order they need it, so they can make your drink as quickly and efficiently as possible.

1. Cup.

The first thing a barista needs to know is what cup to grab for your drink. If you don't specify, we'll put it in our logo cup. But you can also ask for a for-here, iced, or personal cup.

2. Shots and size

Do you want decaf or extra espresso? Here's something to know: Tall (12 fl oz) drinks usually come with one shot; Grande (16 fl oz) drinks have two; Venti drinks have two (for 20 fl oz hot drinks) or three (for 24 fl oz cold drinks). So if you add a shot to your Tall, you're getting a Double Tall.

Syrup.

This is the most popular way to customize. We have many different flavors to sweeten or spice up a drink.

Milk and other modifiers.

This is when you tell us what milk you want. And if you want something else, like "extra hot" or "extra foamy."

The drink itself.

Don't forget the most important part! Are you having a latte, a mocha . . . or something entirely different?

Source: From Make It Your Drink: A Guide to Starbucks Beverages (Seattle, WA: Starbucks Press, 2003).

We love the Starbucks example because it spotlights the attributes of a good customer-training experience: quick, easy, and palatable, if not downright fun. Your training program has to feel good to customers, whose tolerance for discomfort is reliably low, despite any well-earned fantasies you might have of becoming *Seinfeld*'s iconic Soup Nazi, a service provider who gets his customers to behave by screaming at them.

Customers generally aren't willing to give up their dignity as a cost of your service, unless your soup really is that good. There's a reason the following scene from *Seinfeld* was considered wonderfully ridiculous:

ELAINE: Why? What happens if you don't order right?

JERRY: He yells and you don't get your soup.

ELAINE: What?

JERRY: Just follow the ordering procedure and you will be fine.

GEORGE: All right. All right. Let's—let's go over that again.

JERRY: All right. As you walk in the place move immediately to your right.

ELAINE: What?

JERRY: The main thing is to keep the line moving.

GEORGE: All right. So, you hold out your money, speak your soup in a loud, clear voice, step to the left and receive.

JERRY: Right. It's very important not to embellish on your order. No extraneous comments. No questions. No compliments.

ELAINE: Oh, boy, I'm really scared![3]

Most companies can't afford to intimidate their customers. Nor can they afford to confuse them. Toy manufacturers push this boundary all the time with complicated instruction manuals for assembling Junior's tricycle. That's not a training strategy with longevity in mind, which may be appropriate for an industry with sky-high customer turnover (how many tricycles will you buy in a lifetime?). But most organizations need their customers to come back, and so making them crazy is bad for business.

When one global telecom company we studied launched its Internet service, it did a full-scale rollout of a self-install system that had been piloted with employees. The company sent out disks with what it thought were perfectly clear installation instructions, then was alarmed to discover thousands of interpretations of the step-by-step procedure, which varied significantly, depending on the type of computer a customer owned. The company's help lines were quickly overwhelmed. Customer frustration climbed sky high until the company overhauled its customers' role in the installation process, along with the infrastructure to support them.

Customer Job Design

Managers routinely make the same mistake this telecom company did: expecting customers to be as skilled as employees. Some firms place an even larger operational burden on customers than they do on their own employees. As we explored in chapter 2, this happens a lot with self-service models, when untrained customers are suddenly asked to perform the same role that trained employees once did (again, recall the anxiety on the faces of customers in a supermarket self-checkout line). This is in contrast to the empowered travelers swiftly meeting their needs with the simplified tools at an airline check-in kiosk.

We often tell companies that are thinking about giving their customers more work: "Think airline kiosk check-in, not supermarket checkout." It's shorthand for *be deeply thoughtful* about what you're asking your customers to do. LSQ Funding Group used this philosophy when it extended its intuitive IT system to its customers, who now remotely upload the necessary data directly onto the company's servers, in precisely the form LSQ needs to rapidly evaluate the information. Handing this step over to customers helps to reduce the turnaround time of financing, a critical part of the company's value proposition. And it also exposes customers to information that would be otherwise unavailable through conventional methods, such as the credit history and payment performance of their own clients. These are the inputs LSQ uses to evaluate its customers' funding requests, but most customers never see this information. All that most customers typically know is whether their own clients pay them or not. The data helps LSQ's customers to better manage payment risk.

As a result, LSQ's self-service model is preferable to the full-service alternative. But it only works because the system is easy for customers to understand and use—and because a powerful incentive is built into its customer management system. The faster and more accurate the performance of LSQ's customer-operators, the sooner they get their money.

eBay takes the customer-operator role to an extreme, placing customers in all the core roles in a traditional retail environment—advertising, merchandising, ordering, fulfillment, and shipping. Many of its customer service functions are even staffed by other customers, such as peer-to-peer user forums, where experienced sellers coach the novices. Even quality control is outsourced to customers via an elaborate system of feedback stars. With hundreds of millions of customers, the sheer number of customer-operators is one of eBay's distinct challenges, but the company got it right by using transaction software that's highly intuitive and by designing an interface that's simple and pleasant to use. The tasks are straightforward, even for the customer who collects antique teacups but who resents the crassness of modern technology. And for anyone who has trouble keeping up, the system offers cheerful reminders of the correct operating behavior each step of the way. We call this approach *innovating with empathy.*

Magazine Luiza: Refusing to Underestimate the Poor

Magazine Luiza is a huge Brazilian retailer—the third-largest in the country—that wins by defying conventional wisdom about the capacity of its customers.[a] The company's success is linked to the customer management system it has designed for its unconventional target market: poor, "unbanked" clients who are often not functionally literate. For the service model to work, particularly in rural areas, the company had to find new ways to train, deploy, and manage its customers—and help them meet many of their own unique needs.

These were nontrivial challenges. Service manuals were useless. Few customers had any previous experience with credit, a problem for a store whose central business was in household appliances. And because many of Magazine Luiza's customers lived in areas of low population density, it made no economic sense for rural stores to carry much in the way of inventory.

But Magazine Luiza was committed to excellence. The solution it delivered had two parts: a stripped-down virtual store combined with an employee-customer mentorship program that introduces clients to the retail experience in a very hands-on way. The virtual store, whose launch costs are 15 percent of a conventional store, has no products on display. It consists of six to eight selling stations, each of which is simply a desk and a computer. Once a transaction is complete, the company guarantees home delivery within forty-eight hours.

Salespeople at the virtual stores work closely with customers, making customers comfortable with viewing merchandise online and with the idea of buying on credit. Employees become one-on-one tutors in the buying process, including explaining to customers the counterintuitive notion of consuming something before it's fully paid for. For low-income buyers in Brazil, this idea sounds ridiculous. But it's the gateway to other forms of financial empowerment, including personal loans and insurance policies, which Magazine Luiza also began to offer in partnership with Unibanco. These kinds of services were out of reach to most of its customers until the company got into the business.

Because so many prospective purchasers are not skilled readers, the emphasis of the virtual store is on Q&A and pictures. Every appliance can be seen in at least ten different images, and from almost every imaginable angle (including underneath). Once customer-operators are trained in their role (educating themselves about products, creating customized credit terms), they're off and running with the store's self-service tools, with minimal need for their employee coaches. Employees now get to focus on the rest of the service experience, which includes celebrating transactions with in-store parties. A purchase on the scale of a refrigerator or television is often an unprecedented achievement for the customers.

Of all the company's sales, 80 percent are on credit, on terms that are typically more generous than those offered by other Brazilian retailers—and far more generous than the country's credit card companies. The terms are customized to the employment profile of each customer and take into consideration both seasonal trends (e.g., for construction work) and informal sources of income. As part of the deal, customers are required to return to the store each month and make their payments in person. The client response? Magazine Luiza is rewarded with fierce loyalty and a default rate that is 50 percent lower than the average for Brazilian retailers.

Magazine Luiza also works hard to make its customer-operators feel at home in the work environment. To build capacity, commitment, and a sense of belonging, stores often become de facto community centers. Here, clients are the focus of the company's training initiatives.

Magazine Luiza customers get free Internet access and classes ranging from computer literacy to cooking to English. They can also access basic banking services, including access to their bank accounts and utility bill payment.

This expanded offering captures the company's unique strategy, which layers high levels of consumer empathy and innovation on top of a sustainable cost structure. It's a recipe for exceptional success. What started out as a small mom-and-pop store in the rural interior of Brazil has grown, under CEO Luiza Helena Trajano's leadership, to a chain of over two hundred stores and six thousand employees. It carries thousands of products and, in recent years, has delivered as much as a 35 percent return on equity.

Magazine Luiza is managing its customer-operators in unprecedented ways, which has created the economic opening for excellence. The alternative to the virtual store, after all, is no store at all, since traditional retail economics don't work in places where the company's customers live. The retailer has smashed through the barriers to consumption for poor consumers, who are otherwise excluded from the market for household goods and financial services.

a. Material adapted from Todd Benson, "Courting the Poor, a Retailer Rises to No. 3 in Brazil," *New York Times,* July 14, 2004; and Frances X. Frei and Ricardo Reisen de Pinho, "Magazine Luiza: Building a Retail Model of 'Courting the Poor,'" Case 9–606-048 (Boston: Harvard Business School, 2005).

Innovating without empathy rarely delivers the same kinds of results, particularly when it comes to customer-operators. Technology makes it possible to dramatically expand the customer's operating role, but that doesn't necessarily translate into better numbers. Many banks learned this the hard way in the 1990s. As retail banks increased the number of low-cost channels for customers to use to serve themselves—voice-recognition systems, ATMs, online banking—the institutions inadvertently undermined their margins. That's because customers didn't necessarily migrate to the lower-cost solutions. Instead, many simply increased their numbers of transactions overall, still coming to the teller window to deposit their weekly paychecks while also hitting the ATM and checking their balance online. In some cases, these high-tech tools enabled customers to engage their finances at a deeper level, which then *increased* their demand for traditional, high-cost banking services.[4]

Here's the irony: these banks were trying to save money with online tools, but instead, they designed a more costly model. Customers became much more expensive to serve, which wasn't sustainable. When your goal is service excellence, we suggest taking the opposite approach.

Customer job design, especially self-service design, works best when you first work to increase the quality of the service experience, to make the service more convenient or customized (or whatever drives value in your business). Then consider costs. This was LSQ's approach—customers got financing faster by working a little bit harder, which also happened to save the company time and money.

Managing Customer Performance

Customer-operators shouldn't be left entirely on their own, any more than employees should. Unscrupulous customers trying to sell counterfeit products or engage in other fraudulent activities are the bane of eBay. Rather than screen prospective sellers, the online retailer developed an extensive system of oversight, relying primarily on ratings provided by other customers.

Companies regularly try to encourage customer cooperation through discounts and late fees, often with frustrating results. The Blockbuster business model was highly dependent on customer compliance, meaning Katie or Kareem had to leave the comforts of home to ensure that high-demand DVDs got back on the shelf in time for rapid circulation. It was an uphill battle, particularly since studies keep showing that instrumental methods such as fines for being late actually give consumers a sense of entitlement. "OK, I'm compensating the company for my transgression," many conclude. "It's a fair exchange."

Netflix overcame the customer operating problems that had plagued Blockbuster. The newer company accomplished this by setting up an entirely new service model with different offerings, protocols, and incentives. Central to the model was a customer-operator role that required little persuasion or enforcement. The Netflix customer pays a monthly fee to keep a certain number of DVDs in circulation. The moment you send one back, the company automatically sends you another one, keeping your supply of disks at the level of your contract. But you can't get more without returning what you have, a powerful incentive to send the inventory back. More recently, of course, Netflix introduced point-and-click downloads, instant gratification with minimal need for compliance controls.

Using business model innovation to eliminate the difficult compliance step that was plaguing Blockbuster, Netflix basically demoted its customer-operators. Rather than driving across town to the video store by a specific date and time (a hard task), all you had to do was now stroll to your mailbox at your convenience (an easy task). What if demotion is not an option for your business? Psychologists would discourage you from punishing customers for their bad behavior. Instead, they'd point you in the direction of what they call *normative methods:* the use of shame, blame, and pride to motivate positive behavior. This approach turns out to be far more effective for customers, but it's often harder to design and manage.

The Values Lever

Zipcar, the popular car-sharing company, operates in a world in which customer compliance—in this case cleaning, refueling, and returning cars in time for the next user—remains absolutely critical. Many observers assumed that these kinds of service model challenges would keep the company from growing beyond a niche offering for a small segment of dedicated "green" consumers in the Northeastern United States. They were wrong. Ten years after its launch in 2000, Zipcar is the largest car-sharing service in the world. It claims over half a million customers in twenty-eight states in the United States and Canada, and its European expansion is going strong. The company's initial public offering in 2011 raised almost $175 million, far more than expected.

Here's how it works: for an annual fee, zipsters, as members are called, obtain an access card with a wireless chip, which entitles them to go online and reserve a car months or minutes in advance. Zipcar gives them a location where they will find the agreed-upon vehicle waiting at a special Zipcar parking space. Swipe the appropriate access card over a transponder in the windshield, the car doors open, the keys are inside, and away you go. You then return a clean, gassed-up car to the agreed-upon space at an agreed-upon time.

And therein lies the rub. The Zipcar Web site describes it as "a real drag" when members don't do their part and fail to return the car by the agreed-upon deadline—but "a real drag" may be an understatement. The Zipcar service model doesn't have the latitude of a Hertz or an Avis, where customers come to a central facility that has dozens of cars, including a healthy number of unclaimed spares. Zipcar employs a service design in which a single, specific car is supposed to be waiting for a specific user at a specific street corner at a specific time. There are no attendants to gas up, wash, and vacuum, or to make sure that the kind of car you requested is actually sitting in slot 29B when you arrive. The Zipcar system is entirely dependent on the previous customer-operator's adherence to the rules. Subtracting from the available wiggle room, this is a service in which many users are renting for only an hour or two and, as likely as not, for time-sensitive errands. To have a job interview in a distant suburb in one hour and to find yourself on a street corner staring at an empty parking space, where you expected to find your means of transportation, is more than "a real drag."[5]

Zipcar exacts a $50 per hour fine for returning a car late, but again, late fees tend to mitigate guilt and thus enable bad behavior. The more promising (normative) method is to create an environment that will induce customer-operators to care about the effects of their behavior on others. Fortunately for Zipcar, prosocial behavior is very much in keeping with its progressive brand and the values of its target demographic. So in addition to fees, Zipcar works hard to remind you that you're joining a community with clear obligations to other members of the community *who are just like you.* Rather than buying the service from cold-blooded capitalists, you're supposed to think about Zipcar leaders as "idea people" and "ambassadors for change."[6] The company also hosts regular social events to introduce you to your fellow community members in a relaxed setting where human connections can be made. It turns out it's easier to sabotage the travel plans of an anonymous person than to mess with that cool zipster you met playing pool the other night.

This is where organizational culture very much rears its head. As we'll explore in chapter 5, culture makes an enormous difference to employee performance. But it can matter just as much for customers, particularly in service companies, where customers are highly exposed to firm operations. That's why culture is an equal factor in our uncommon service equation:

$$\text{Service Excellence} = \text{Design} \times \text{Culture}$$

Zipcar uses culture to help manage its customers by making its values highly visible, infusing every customer interaction with the "we're all in this together" mentality that's so critical to its business model. Magazine Luiza makes the same choice. The ambition and enthusiasm the company cultivates in its employees spills over to its customers, which is part of what makes the model so appealing to disenfranchised consumers, whose humanity is not always embraced by other formal institutions. Shouldice Hospital's core belief that recovery should be fast, active, and social provides the cultural foundation for the patient experience. Keep this in mind when you start to diagnose and strengthen the culture of your own company: employees aren't your only target. By inviting customers to play an operating role in your business, you're also inviting them to be influenced by your organization's worldview.

CASE STUDY

Killing Bugs with BBBK Customers

To say that customer-operators were central to the value proposition at Bugs Burger Bug Killers is almost a laughable understatement. That radical guarantee of complete pest elimination? It would have been empty without customers who were willing to toil alongside the company to ensure that their own restaurants, hotels, and apartment buildings were highly inhospitable to critters.

In order to deliver uncommon service, BBBK needed its customers to not just work hard, but also to perform difficult steps in the company's rigorous antibug protocol. And so the company pulled out all the stops to keep its customers on point. Before the very first service visit, customers had to agree in writing to a strict cleanup regimen. No agreement, no deal—it was a powerful customer-selection tool. Next, the company developed a specific action plan for each client. This plan often involved more frequent cleanups, radical changes in trash management, and not-so-cheap repairs to the building and surrounding site. If customers did not cooperate, they were fined. If they still didn't cooperate, they were unceremoniously dropped. As Bugs himself declared over and over again, "We don't want to do business with them."

Customer training was a central part of the service specialist's role. BBBK employees spent as much time as needed with the client to make sure the protocol and action plan were clear. Early site visits were as much about coaching customers as treating the facility. A typical learning moment for a client went something like this: a BBBK team would throw any piles of junk it found onto the middle of a client's floor, then place a sign on the pile: "Sorry for the Mess." And then the real learning occurred. When a customer approached the sign, he or she would find the following message: "Please accept my apology for the mess I made. I had to make the choice of doing one of two things. (1) Leave things as they were, cluttered and dirty, allowing roaches or rodents to infest your establishment again; or (2) Break up the breeding area. I chose number two because I know you don't want to lose our guarantees and have an infestation of roaches or rodents again."[a]

The demands that BBBK placed on its customer-operators were unprecedented in the bug business—or in any other business we've studied, at least for sheer degree of difficulty. The *Washington Post* documented a BBBK intervention for one D.C. customer: "Preparing for Burger's bug men was almost like getting ready for a visit from a mother-in-law who would be sure to find any speck of dust. The aftermath was also exhausting: three people spend five hours mopping up filmy pesticide residue and putting the place back together."[b] For many clients, BBBK's process also meant lost operating hours during the initial cleanup phase, which could sometimes be measured in days.

But there was no other route to excellence. It turns out that customers who wanted the best were more than willing to do their part.

a. Content on BBBK is derived from William E. Fulmer, "Bugs Burger Bug Killers, Inc. (A)," Case 9–694-018 (Used by Harvard Business School with permission of William E. Fulmer). Fulmer's sources include Tom Richman, "Getting the Bugs Out," *Inc.,* June 1984; Annette Kornblum, "Bugs Burger," *Pest Control,* November 1980; and Joan Livingston, "Absolutely Guaranteed," *Nation's Business,* November 1987. All quotations are taken from this case.

b. Annette Kornblum, "Of Mice, Men and Roaches: Bugs Burger's Philosophy," *Washington Post,* July 5, 1981.

Putting It into Practice

We tend to think of managing customers in phases. First, you need to get control. Find out how your customers are influencing the cost and quality of your service today, and then nudge them in a better direction. In our experience, almost all service organizations can benefit from some version of this exercise, if only to bring sunlight and confidence to your assumptions. Even the most basic of assumptions can turn out to be startlingly wrong when it comes to customer operating behavior.

The next phase involves actively deploying customer-operators, but in a targeted way. Get them to help you improve your current processes, for example, or add customers to the design team as you start mapping out a new service offering. This is the walk-but-not-run phase, the first tentative steps toward tapping the operating value of your customer base. Start to blur the boundaries between employees and customers.

The final phase is what we call going all the way, embracing your customers as very central producers of the services you provide. Think of it as the eBay way. This phase carries tremendous potential upside. And a meaningful amount of risk.

Let's look at these three phases in more detail.

Phase 1: Getting Control

You have lots of ways to measure—and therefore improve—your effectiveness in managing employees: utilization, turnover, evaluations, rate of advancement. But how do you know how you're doing with customer-operators? How do you know if your job design or management strategies are producing the behaviors you want? Or if the behaviors you're promoting are actually the right ones?

Sometimes you can trust your gut or gather anecdotal feedback to get a sense of the story. First Union Bank made a reasonable assumption that low adoption of its self-service channels reflected low customer awareness. Maybe customers just didn't know that the ATM was an option. So the company hired spunky greeters to direct customers to lower-cost ATM channels as they entered the bank. The effort backfired. It turned out that First Union customers actively preferred to use tellers, for a wide range of reasons, and the company's attempt to dissuade them caused widespread resentment. It got so bad that the *Philadelphia Inquirer* ran a series of stories on poor service at the bank, highlighting customers such as Steven Fischer, who declared that First Union had deeply offended him: "[The bank] has alienated me. They have insulted my intelligence."[7]

The scowls on the faces of First Union's customers were enough of a tip-off that the company's assumptions were wrong. But the truth is often buried deeper than where your intuition can reach. Uncovering it starts with the willingness to stop treating your beliefs as facts. Banks assumed that since online channels were cheaper to operate than offline channels, then online adoption would lead to cost savings. The logic made so much sense that no one bothered to test it.

The most painful part of this story is that testing it would have been very straightforward. The relevant data was already being collected, and the analysis wasn't complicated. The hard part was reframing the certainties in managers' minds as hypotheses that needed confirmation. It turns out that this is the hard part in most organizations. And for whatever reason, this is particularly true for customer behavior. At the risk of sounding melodramatic, we would suggest that there's an epidemic of overconfidence in service companies when it comes to predicting the operating behavior of their customers. Fortunately, the treatment is cheap and effective: surface your operating assumptions. Get in touch with whatever conclusions you've reached about the impact of customers on your operations. Now test your assumptions with data you probably already have.

Phase 2: Actively Involving Customers

As a taste of what's possible, we offer the simplest, lowest-risk way to get your customers to help you operationally: bring them into your improvement process. Here we take inspiration from the world of manufacturing. One of many things that distinguished Toyota's celebrated production system was something called an *andon cord,* which was suspended from the ceiling in front of every worker on the assembly line. Any time someone on the line saw a problem, he or she was obligated to pull the cord, which cued flashing lights and music. A manager instantly came over to investigate, and unless the manager pulled the cord again right away, everything stopped until the quality flaw was fixed. Later, the employee with the sharp eye was celebrated, on the theory that finding a problem today creates an opportunity to be better tomorrow.[8]

In the world of the customer-operator, the analog to the andon cord is the customer complaint. We've studied patterns in complaint letters and e-mails, which give you a fascinating window into how businesses manage their customers and whether companies view customers as operating assets. A generic response sends a clear message, as does detailed engagement from the chief operating officer. Not responding at all—a notorious habit of a shocking number of industries—sends another kind of signal.

Most companies try to buy off the customer and reduce the chance that he or she will talk trash about them. A service team is deployed to apologize profusely and offer free things to shut the customer up, but that's typically where the process ends. This is a missed opportunity. By treating complaints simply as service recovery moments, companies miss the improvement opportunities piling up in their mailrooms and on their servers. The things that make managing customer-operators so difficult (their sheer numbers and diversity) also make them an incredible resource for refining your service model. Ask your frontline employees to stop buffering you from these calls and letters, even if it's just for a week or two. What patterns do you see? How do your customers feel about their operating role? What are the systematic opportunities for improvement?

Phase 3: Going All the Way

Despite the complexities of managing customer-operators, companies are intrigued by the idea—and some are down for the count. Many organizations today want to give customers a more meaningful role to play in their operations, and some businesses are ready to go all the way. If you find yourself ready to take the plunge, there are some important things to keep in mind.

In 2009, Scott Cook, CEO of Intuit, wrote a fantastic article, "The Contribution Revolution: Let Volunteers Build Your Business."[9] His insight was to build on the idea of the company-hosted, online support forum common among software and computer companies. Most people have a natural inclination to be helpful. And when you're dealing with the number of things that can go wrong when installing a router, the chances of finding a solution will dramatically increase when you tap into the collective wisdom of thousands of fellow users, rather than rely exclusively on your paid employees.

Cook challenges his readers to take the logical next step, to involve your customers in all kinds of functions. His examples are great and foreshadow a brave, new world where all kinds of companies think creatively about how to harness their customers' talent and effort. *Wikipedia* is the classic web-based model. The online encyclopedia has relied almost entirely on far-flung volunteers to create a body of knowledge that experts say is about as accurate as *Encyclopedia Britannica,* while covering a far greater range of subjects. But old-school companies are now jumping into the game. Hyatt Hotels and Resorts has an online concierge service that aggregates information and lets users rate travel tips posted by both customers and professional concierges. Procter & Gamble has a Web site called BeingGirl.com, which allows teens to share their questions and experiences in the context of feminine hygiene products. P&G says that as a marketing tool, BeingGirl.com is four times as effective, dollar for dollar, as television advertising.

As we've revealed, we agree wholeheartedly with Cook's premise. There can be tremendous advantages to getting your customers to help you create the value they ultimately consume. But more is not always more. One of the reasons to involve a customer is to foster a sense of ownership, which brings with it a level of commitment and energy that's good for everyone. The fierce loyalty of heavy eBay sellers makes the experience better for all stakeholders, since these prolific sellers drive company growth while protecting its culture and community standards. But once you give your customers a seat at the table, you have to be sure you're ready to deal with them there.

Threadless is an apparel company that made a splash by bringing its clients into the design process.[10] Customers were allowed to vote on T-shirt designs submitted by amateurs, and the winning concepts were then produced and marketed. This worked beautifully in the sense that it reduced R&D costs as well as unsold inventory, because the designs were inherently in sync with the buyers' taste. The problem arose when Threadless began to consider a corporate merger, and its customer base went crazy. A sense of ownership, in this case, translated into a demand for decision rights about firm-level strategy. Threadless ultimately backed away from the merger, in part because it didn't want to alienate its customers.

When customers have meaningful operating control, their level of investment can take companies by surprise. eBay confronted this tension when it decided to do something as seemingly benign as change the color of the site's feedback stars. Customers called for revolution. The manager who made the decision was relatively new, and it never occurred to her to check with customers about such a basic operating decision.

An Ode to Customer-Operators

Whether you're giving your customers a starring role in your operations or you simply don't have a choice but to bring them around, our message is essentially the same. On the path to excellence, every company has to change its customers' behavior at some point along the way. Sometimes it's a big change, and sometimes it's minor, but every successful service business confronts this challenge. When you find yourself at that inflection point, you have two choices: get your customers to behave differently and have them hate you for it ("Push six for sales, four for service"), or get them to behave differently and like you even *more* for it. Great companies pull off option number two.

UNCOMMON TAKEAWAYS

✓ Service customers don't just purchase a service; they also participate in creating it. Among other things, they make the service faster or slower, better or worse, cheaper or more expensive to deliver—for themselves and for other customers. They are active producers (and detractors) of the value they end up consuming.

✓ For example, a customer at a salad bar affects the quality of his or her meal, whereas patients who skip dental appointments drive up the costs of running the entire practice. When customers are influencing the service experience in ways like these, we call them *customer-operators.*

✓ Customers can be more or less involved operationally, depending on your industry and on your specific design choices—for example, how much self-service you build into your model and whether you involve your customers in your improvement efforts.

✓ The more dependent your service business is on the behavior of customer-operators, the more important it is to manage them successfully. Similar to employee management, the four components of a successful customer management system are customer selection, training, job design, and performance management.

✓ Not all customer-operators are alike. When compared with each other, they are faster, slower, smarter, pickier, later, earlier, or more or less prepared to perform their operational roles. This diversity increases the cost and complexity of running a service business.

✓ Assume that you don't know exactly how your customers are affecting your operations or how well your efforts to manage them are really going. Reframe any certainties as hypotheses that need confirmation. Test them. Fortunately, the data you need is usually right at your fingertips.

Chapter Five

Now Multiply
It All by Culture

Imagine yourself walking around an empty building. The lay-out is intuitive, each room surrendering easily to the next one. You feel strangely reassured, even optimistic. You sit down on a bench that you hadn't really noticed before, but which suddenly seems to be in exactly the right place. And you find yourself lingering, again an unfamiliar impulse. You feel the volume of the noise in your mind start to lower. That's the *feeling* of great design.

When a service model is designed right, it produces the same sensations among the people who interact with it—energy, reassurance, the sense of calm that comes from being deeply respected as a living being. But like an empty building, a well-designed service model is still missing the critical element that brings it to life on a functional level: the people, or more specifically, how the people interact with each other. When we're talking about organizations, we call that element *culture*.

A great service organization needs to get both right, the service design and the culture that animates it. Both must be pointing in the same direction, toward the outputs you've identified as critical to your organization's success. Let's put it this way—if you go to work in that beautiful building, and your boss is a tyrant, or even just indifferent to your needs, it doesn't matter that the bench was in exactly the right place. All that structural genius goes to waste in an environment where the rules of engagement produce the exact opposite emotions.

Equality at Ten Thousand Feet

For a taste of what we mean, let's revisit our now-familiar airline service model: Southwest Airlines. The key to Southwest's service model is faster gate turnaround than its competitors, which allows the company to get more flying time out of its high-cost, airborne assets and therefore to charge customers less to get somewhere. Pulling off its signature turnaround times requires an exceptionally high level of collaboration across specialists, levels, and functions. And so Southwest is all about ego-free cooperation. No one is better than anyone else. No one is above doing what needs to be done. Everyone is equal in the Southwest universe—an ethos that extends to passengers, who until recently couldn't even buy their way to business class if they wanted to.

Among the most visible expressions of this egalitarian culture is an institution called "team late." If the plane arrives late, everyone is penalized, and so everyone pitches in with whatever needs to happen, without having to be told.[1] This performance measure makes sense, of course, given the airline's operating imperatives. But it's in the less transparent decisions where Southwest's cultural consistency really stands out. Southwest has a greater number of unionized employees than any other airline, yet it also has better employee relations than any other airline. Why isn't that a contradiction? It turns out that unions love Southwest because, unlike other airlines, it has never had a layoff. Southwest didn't expand as much as traditional airlines did during good times, which means that it doesn't need to cut back quite so much during bad times. This policy is designed to maintain good employee relationships, and it is these good relationships that allow Southwest to include the team-late provision in employment contracts, as well as put the phrase "and everything else" into all of Southwest's job descriptions. Whatever needs doing, you simply do it, without having to locate, for instance, a qualified master electrician to screw in a light bulb. And this chain of interlocking trade-offs—expansion limits to preserve job stability in return for flexibility in job descriptions—all leads directly to faster turnaround, the key to Southwest's success.

The Mad, Mad Logic of IDEO

Culture may be an organization's most important part that you can't actually see. As the invisible foundation that runs underneath everything else, culture is more difficult to diagnose. One way to start is by looking at the way culture manifests in an organization's visible choices and behaviors, the tangible by-products—the *stuff*—of culture. No one makes this stuff easier to observe than IDEO, the global design firm.

IDEO has developed everything from the first Apple mouse to the twenty-five-foot mechanical whale for the movie *Free Willy.* The company gained an even higher profile when

ABC's *Nightline* did a segment on its design of a new kind of shopping cart in only four days. The final design had a price scanner, hooks for hanging bags, wheels that could better handle the tight corners inside stores, and no central basket, so that it would be less of a temptation for thieves.

We love the story of IDEO, pedagogically, because you can really touch and feel what's distinct about IDEO's culture—and intuitively see why it matters.[2] Creativity is IDEO's lifeblood. Nothing is more important to its business model. So how does the company create an environment where creative excellence is a consistently probable outcome? Certainly, IDEO relies on good service model design—in particular, its employee management system. The company looks for well-understood attributes in the targeting and selection of new hires—attributes that signal the ability to both innovate and inspire innovation in others. But what allows this team to deliver day after day, year after year, is the culture that these individuals are subsequently thrown into. It's the company's service design multiplied by its culture.

Signs of that culture are unnerving to the traditional corporate eye. IDEO has no dress code. Employees create their own ad hoc workspaces out of plastic cubes. In the center of the office is a celebrated institution called the Tech Box, a tripped-out salvage yard of industrial design—bits of Kevlar, odd hinges and switches and balls that don't bounce, an archery bow based on pulleys—that employees regularly rummage through for inspiration.

What's so different about a day in the life of IDEO? Consider brainstorming. Storming the brains of its employees is a huge part of the company's process and a big part of each day. The process is crafted to encourage wild ideas and defer judgment until a later stage. It's also designed to build on the ideas of others without concern for credit, to hold only one conversation at a time to make sure the introverts participate, and to maximize quantity of ideas (sometimes 150 in under an hour) rather than getting too hung up on quality in the beginning. After these sessions, discarded ideas are archived—just in case.

"Rough, rapid, and right," is a company motto, but "right" refers to getting specific parts of the design right. There is no pressure for anyone to *be* right or to find the answer early on, which would inhibit the free expression of ideas. "Failure is part of the culture," founder and CEO David Kelley told *Research Technology Management.* "We call it enlightened trial and error."[3] There are lots of failures, even late in the process, but Kelley insists that IDEO learns just as much from a model that's wrong as from one that moves the company clearly in the right direction.

The experience of collective creativity is most intense during Deep Dive, when the team spends a whole day intently focused on generating a large number of creative concepts, weeding out the weak ideas, and moving on to prototypes of the several best solutions. "Fail often to succeed sooner," a process that can look to outsiders like wasting time, is an IDEO conviction. As is working hard. Motivation is spurred to the level of sixty-hour weeks by the shared enthusiasm of your colleagues (read: peer pressure). There's also nowhere for non-contributors to hide in the company's small, borderless studio workspace.

And it all happens through temporary teams and hierarchy. Teams form for the life of the project. There are few if any permanent job titles or assignments. Staffers keep their personal stuff in portable bookcases so they can move easily among projects. Leadership is often based on personal excitement or facilitation skills—not on seniority. Employee assessment is done by peer review, with peers chosen by the employee being evaluated. High levels of contribution are rewarded with opportunities to work on the most interesting projects.

Again, we bring up all these things because they are the visible components of IDEO's culture. They are the outward expressions of the company's underlying norms and values—take risks, move fast, play is important—a phenomenon that MIT culture scholar Edgar Schein describes as an organization's "artifacts" and "espoused values" (which we call behaviors).[4] They are the things an outside observer can see as different about what happens at IDEO. But other companies could eliminate their dress code, put a pile of junk in the middle of the reception area, and declare that no idea is a bad idea. This would have little effect, of course, except to confuse the visitors.

Why it works at IDEO—and what allows the company to churn out excellence at a regular clip—are what Schein calls the "shared basic assumptions" that drive all of these seemingly odd choices. If you want to change culture, then you have to start there, by influencing the thought patterns that drive your employees to act.

Building Blocks of Culture

There are great thinkers in the organizational behavior domain that can walk you through the latest research on culture and human psychology. We are not those people. We do recommend *Hidden Value: Getting Extraordinary Results with Or-*

dinary People, by Charles O'Reilly and Jeff Pfeffer,[5] as well as Amy Edmondson's research on organizations that create psychological safety for their employees,[6] which is some of the most exciting work we've seen in this space. There are many others who deserve to be on that list.

Our starting point is operations, and so we bring a very practical orientation to these questions. We want to know *how* a culture of service excellence is built, what happens differently inside companies that achieve this elusive goal. One of our favorite practical examples is from the service turnaround efforts at Ochsner Health System's Baton Rouge clinic. When we asked Baton Rouge CEO Mitch Wasden what he thought the most important driver of significant cultural change has been, he pointed to the 5-10 rule. All employees are now asked to visually acknowledge anyone within ten feet of them and to verbally acknowledge anyone within five feet. This seemingly small change has made a remarkable difference in the urgent, time-sensitive clinic setting, where everyone has an important job to do quickly. Now part of that job is to pause and acknowledge the humanity of the people around you—patients, colleagues, the UPS delivery guy—by following a simple, but powerful rule: say hello.

These kinds of practical tools for communicating and reinforcing culture show up across organizations that consistently deliver outstanding customer value. More specifically, we've seen three distinct patterns in these organizations' relationship to culture. All demonstrate high levels of the following:

- *Clarity:* knowing exactly what kind of a culture you want to build, and how this culture is critical to achieving your most important performance objectives

- *Signaling:* relentlessly communicating the organization's core values, particularly in moments when people are likely to be most receptive to these messages, such as during recruiting and orientation

- *Consistency:* reinforcing the culture at every turn and rooting out *cultural violations,* that is, misalignment between the desired culture and organizational strategy, structure, and operations

Zappos, the fantastically successful online shoe retailer, is particularly good at all three. We'll now look at how Zappos and others used these cultural levers to help build uncommon service companies.

Clarity: Know Where You're Going

Zappos will take an order as late as midnight and deliver it to the customer's doorstep before breakfast. It has the world's largest selection of shoes, and its service includes free returns. If it doesn't have the shoe you want in stock or in your size, a Zappos call center employee will go to three competitors' sites to try to help you locate what you want to buy. Seventy-five percent of its business comes from repeat customers, despite the fact that its prices are far from the lowest. (Price is an area where Zappos has made a conscious trade-off in its service model in order to deliver exceptional service.)

It's not surprising, then, that managers from other companies—including many from service and quality leaders like

Southwest and Toyota—make regular pilgrimages to Zappos facilities to learn how the company pulls it off. Everyone wants to know what the heck is going on. A quick look around reveals that part of its success is the company's IT strategy, including a real-time inventory management system that is 99 percent accurate, compared with accuracy rates as low as 40 percent in other areas of retail. But what gets visitors every time are the clues to Zappos's true competitive advantage: its culture. And no one inside the company is surprised.

The most visible champion of Zappos's culture, naturally enough, is president and CEO Tony Hsieh (pronounced "Shay"). Hsieh is crystal clear on the culture he needs to make the company thrive, and he and his team have broken it down into ten core company values:

1. Deliver *wow* through service.

2. Embrace and drive change.

3. Create fun and a little weirdness.

4. Be adventurous, creative, and open-minded.

5. Pursue growth and learning.

6. Build open and honest relationships with communication.

7. Build a positive team and family spirit.

8. Do more with less.

9. Be passionate and determined.

10. Be humble.[7]

Hsieh embodies these values. He is passionate, positive, fun, humble. And a little weird. As the fearless leader of a high-profile shoe company, Hsieh unapologetically wore the same pair of shoes every single day for two years. He then replaced them with the exact same pair. Hsieh's definition of weird, however, is closer to authentic or real. He's betting that the "real you" will be more valuable to Zappos than the safe, watered-down version that usually shows up in a work environment. So go ahead, be a little weird.

Early in his career, Hsieh had a breakthrough about how much culture mattered to the performance and motivation of employees. He sold a software company he had founded when he realized that even he no longer wanted to come to work, primarily because of the culture. Now Hsieh does many things you'd expect from an enlightened CEO, like taking calls at the call center on holidays to give his employees a break and staying in direct touch with his customers.

But what really sets Hsieh and his team apart is their deep awareness that culture is the company's most important asset. "Service is a by-product of culture," says former chief financial officer Alfred Lin, as are things like supplier behavior and employee turnover. In 2005, when the company's call center moved from the Bay Area to Las Vegas, an astonishing 80 percent of its California employees relocated—for a $13-an-hour job. In 2008, a year in which the average turnover at call centers was 150 percent, turnover at Zappos was 39 percent (including turnover owing to promotions). Managers attribute the loyalty to a culture that cultivates the passion, purpose, and humanity of its employees.

But it's not just management that gets it. The conviction that culture is key is embraced throughout the ranks at Zappos. It's so central to the company's belief system, in fact, that the company publishes the *Zappos Culture Book*, which is updated regularly and contains hundreds of unscripted comments and essays written by Zappos employees *and vendors* about the company's culture, why it matters, and how it affects what they do every day. It was conceived as a training tool for new hires and partners, but consumption of the book has gone way beyond that internal circle. Ringing in at 348 pages in the 2009 edition, it's a moving and persuasive testament to the power of employee engagement ("happiness" in Zappos-speak), and the role of culture in eliciting it. We recommend buying it and just paging through.

Here's a taste, from Abbie "Abster" M., an employee who had been working at the company for three-plus years:

> *The Zappos culture to me is unlike anything I've ever experienced before. It's always fun and weird, we're all creative and open-minded, passionate and determined, but most of all, we're humble. I think it's because most of us have worked in horrible dead-end jobs before and can cherish our Zappos culture for what it is. It's what makes me want to come to work every day, even my weekends.*
>
> *. . . I hear so many horror stories from friends about the places they work and it only makes me feel that much more fortunate to be a part of the Zappos family. I can't imagine my life without Zappos, and the amazing people that I work with.[8]*

The quote that moved us most was from Ryan A.: "At my last job I was afraid to be anything: right, wrong, smarter, dumber . . . At Zappos being yourself is the best thing you can do."[9] Perhaps the cultural feature we observe most often is unproductive fear, fear of looking bad or doing something wrong. If organizations did nothing else but address that part of their environment, we're confident that the creativity and engagement of their people would have a real chance of being unleashed. Human beings are not at their best in a defensive, self-distracted crouch.

Hsieh named his book on building Zappos *Delivering Happiness,* but he and his team didn't just deliver happiness for its own sake. Like IDEO's relationship with creativity, Zappos understood that the happiness of its employees, partners, and customers was a deadly serious endeavor, the most reliable route to sustaining excellence in the industry in which Zappos chose to compete. Everyone inside Zappos, from the CEO to the front line, understood the link between its culture of happiness and the company's daily performance. What's the cultural analog in your own business? What's your version of happy?

Scaling Service Culture at Publix

A sticky misperception out there is that a strong service culture is a luxury of small companies without the growth and profitability pressure that the big boys have to endure. The commitment to serve is for hobby businesses.

Publix Super Markets blows up this assumption in magnificent ways. A *Fortune* 500 company, Publix is one of the biggest supermarket chains in the United States, with annual revenues in the $25 billion range. The company employs more than 150,000 employees, the vast majority at the low end of the wage scale. And the passion for service that led founder George Jenkins to open his first store in 1930 has been internalized across more than one thousand Publix locations today. Publix consistently scores higher than any other supermarket on the American Customer Satisfaction Index.

Even outside the supermarket category, the number of service accolades heaped onto this company is impressive: Customer's Choice Award (National Retail Federation Foundation), Top 10 Companies That Treat You Right (MSN Money-Zogby), and Top 25 Customer Service Champs (*BusinessWeek*).

How has it pulled off such an exceptional service culture at this scale? An important part of making sure everyone "gets it" is the Publix guarantee:

> We will never knowingly disappoint you. If for any reason your purchase does not give you complete satisfaction, the full purchase price will be cheerfully refunded immediately upon your request.

These words are emblazoned everywhere a Publix employee looks. They're on the walls of stores. They're even printed on the back of every business card of every employee, all the way to the very top of the organization. And the careful selection of words—from the "cheerfully" and "immediately" to the commitment to never intentionally disappoint—makes exactly what the company stands for palpable to everyone who puts on a Publix name tag.

The guarantee is not a mission statement that lives and dies in a glossy annual report. It's alive and well, guiding employees toward the right behavior, even in situations that are confronting them (and the company) for the first time. This was true for Jim Rhodes, who started out as a meat manager in one store and, thirty years later, is now working as vice president of human resources for all of Publix.[a] One day, the president of the company telephoned to deploy him to go handle an irate customer, who was claiming that a frozen Publix pizza had ruined her oven. It was Rhodes's day off, but he put away the lawn mower and jumped into action, arriving at the woman's house within a few minutes. There he discovered a well-used oven that hadn't been cleaned. Ever. The woman had a taste for cooking pizza, preferably right on the baking rack (no pan), and so the accumulation of years of rogue, burnt ingredients had finally caught fire. As Rhodes recalled, "I didn't know anything about customer service." But in that moment, he thought about the guarantee. The guarantee promised complete satisfaction, and so that became his target.

He drove to the store and picked up a few items: two pizzas, baking pan, putty scraper, cans of oven cleaner. And then he got on his knees. And cleaned the woman's oven for her.

It's the same ethos that leads Publix employees to regularly carry packages to customers' cars, to drop off groceries when customers are sick, to *never knowingly disappoint.* Not only has this culture survived in spite of the company's size and success, it has also been the central driver of it. It's a deadly serious asset, cultivated by a soberly ambitious company.

a. This anecdote was documented in Joseph Carvin, *A Piece of the Pie: The Story of Customer Service at Publix* (Nashville, TN: Favorite Recipes Press, 2005), a fantastic resource used to clarify the culture for new Publix employees and share the company's values with the larger business community.

Signaling: Talk the Talk

When he started JetBlue, David Neeleman famously flew as a crew member on his airline once a month.[10] He would put on an apron, serve coffee. "Hi, I'm Dave Neeleman." Every time he did this, he not only electrified passengers on the flight where he was serving, but he also sent a buzz throughout the entire organization. He made it explicit that everyone, at every level, was in service to JetBlue customers. And he signaled that no one, at any level, is above jumping in and doing what needs to be done. The high-profile gesture was also a vivid expression of JetBlue's mission to "bring humanity back to air travel." Seeing the CEO treat a passenger like a human being, introducing himself and asking about the person's needs, was a warning shot to everyone inside and outside the organization that something different was happening on JetBlue flights. No one flies steerage on this airline.

Among the most powerful times to send cultural signals is during your employees' first few days on the job. Psychologists call this phenomenon *imprinting,* the process of deep learning that occurs during certain phases of development, when the brain is more receptive to environmental influences. The behavior was first observed in birds, which, upon hatching, would bond quickly and closely with the first thing they saw.

Even when they were presented with a more "correct" alternative (say, a mother hen instead of the farmer's boot), their preference for the original prevailed. The organizational equivalent is the training experience. In the beginning of a new job, everything is unfamiliar. People's minds are open and eager, working hard to make sense of the things they observe. Whatever they internalize in those first few moments sticks— and, more important, is hard to unstick.

At Commerce Bank, if you recall, within the first ninety seconds, new hires learn that they (1) are part of a crazy tribe of congenitally happy people, (2) have a responsibility to go find others like them, and (3) must answer the phone with an attitude of "Wow!" In these three simple gestures, clocking in at less than two minutes, employees internalize what matters to the company. The firms that hand out binders in the first ninety seconds of orientation—what have they communicated as being important? The bureaucracy?

Companies that really get it start the imprinting process in the recruiting phase. At this point, of course, it's part communication and part alignment. You want to identify people who are likely to be good cultural fits, but you also want to start making it clear what you're all about.

Zappos stands out at this stage, as well. Recruiting at Zappos is an exercise in cultural immersion, with an emphasis on its core value of humility. The process is anchored by two interviews, one for cultural fit, and one for skills, with ten to fifteen behavior-based questions for each.

In the culture interview, the potential hire is asked things like, "Which would you prefer, a ten percent raise or meeting a new friend?" Or, "If you were a superhero, who would you be, and why?" Or, "If you entered a room to a theme song, what would it be?" These questions are designed to reveal useful things about the interviewee, but they are also powerful "speech acts" that send strong signals about the Zappos way of life. You can't make it through the interview without starting to understand it.

Even the skills interview is a somewhat misleading title. Here, culture is still an important part of the agenda. The process includes basic tasks such as typing and Internet navigation, even if you're applying for the job of chief financial officer. "We have recruiting assistants administer the tests," explains recruiting manager Christa Foley. "They test humbleness, as much as the skills themselves. If a candidate is irritated, it is obvious, so this serves as another culture screen." The CFO candidate might be sitting next to a recent high school graduate to take the typing test or, later, during call center training.

The same goes for body language as the candidate tours the facility, another gesture rich in cultural signaling and exposure. The body rarely lies, at least not well. Someone who shows physical discomfort at employees ringing cowbells or multiple parades through the office (just a regular day in the life of Zappos) is revealing something more fundamental than anything he or she might say in an interview.

It actually took Zappos three years to fully staff its finance department, expanding from twelve employees to fifty, in large part because it was difficult to find finance people who fit the culture. If there is someone who might deliver a short-term gain, but who just isn't going to play well on the team, Zappos says no.

Not everyone has to be off the charts in his or her embodiment of the culture, but the person cannot violate any core value. "We don't expect every candidate to match or exhibit each core value in the same way," says Foley. "A new hire may not lead the parade or come up with the idea for it, but they cannot be the person who would roll their eyes at it."

There are deal-breaker questions, such as, "Do you enjoy spending time outside the office with your coworkers?" Managers are expected to spend 20 percent of their time out of the office with their team. And then there's the "weirdness question," the wild card thrown out there just to see how people react. "We want them to laugh at the question," Foley says. "If it bothers them and they get guarded and negative, they are probably not a good fit." A sign of a strong fit, however, is someone who attributes personal success to something other than his or her own ingenuity. "If someone rates themselves as being on the high end of the luck scale, then they are probably going to be the type of person that we're looking for, who will be creative, adventurous, and can think outside of the box," says Foley.

And then—no surprise—Zappos's cultural communications campaign moves seamlessly from recruiting to training. Basic training is four weeks, from 7 a.m. to 4 p.m., Monday through Friday. After the third week, all new employees get The Offer—as described earlier, the $2,000 payoff, no questions asked, to just walk away. Few people do, in part because by this point in the process, they know exactly what they're getting into. If they value the cash more than the opportunity to join Hsieh and his merry band in delivering happiness, then good riddance. All new hires then spend time at the call center, the stomping grounds of the customer loyalty team. After that, it's on to the Incubator, for closely supervised work on the phones.

Each step of the process is relentlessly thoughtful, carefully designed to signal the company's core values and empower people to embrace them. But Alfred Lin shrugs it off as simple: "We only hire happy people and we try to keep them happy." Easy enough, Lin suggests: just hire people who are "inspired by the culture."

CASE STUDY
Storytelling at Sewell Automotive

At Sewell Automotive, the hundred-year-old network of Texas car dealerships famous for its outstanding service, orientation doesn't start with a tour of the office. It starts with story time. New recruits gather around, and a member of the senior team conjures up strange, but true tales of service excellence, narratives that bring Sewell's culture to life in vivid detail.

Some of the stories have been passed down among generations of employees, like when a member of the repair team drove from Dallas to San Antonio in the middle of the night to replace a client's battery. Other stories occurred as recently as the week before, like the other day, when customers kept thanking managers for the flowers, but none of the managers were aware of having given flowers to customers. It turns out it was the cashier's idea. Fresh flowers in the dealership were being tossed at the end of the week, and some of them were still in great shape. Customers might like them, the cashier decided.

Why so many stories?

According to Joe Stallard, vice president of human resources, there are two reasons: to set a clear standard and to give people permission to behave a certain way. It is not, he stresses, to get people to go the extra mile with every service interaction. That's a privilege you have to earn, Stallard emphasizes, and not the foundation of Sewell's service model: "It's not about the extra stuff. It's about consistency. It's about meeting expectations every single time." As a result, many of the stories have a strong reliability theme, or variations on it—keep your word, work hard, be honest with customers and colleagues. These are the cultural values that have kept Sewell at the top of its game for more than a century— even in 1911, when the company was deciding whether to bet on hardware, movie theaters, or a newfangled machine called an automobile.

Like other successful service companies, Sewell has made some critical design choices that reinforce the culture. Recruiting people who embody the company's values is the starting point, Stallard argues, and the company's rigorous recruiting process reflects this belief. Employees must perform exceptionally well in multiple

rounds of interviews and on aptitude and cultural-fit testing. The vast majority are turned away. Sewell's "bias for
smart people" sent its recruiters to college campuses, a
somewhat radical departure for the industry. The company focuses on schools like Texas A&M with shared,
basic assumptions that are similar to Sewell's. Character
is destiny. Service is a privilege.

But it's what happens next that keeps the Sewell
culture strong. Once the cultural training phase (orientation) ends, the people who get it right are very publicly
celebrated through rewards and recognition. Employees
who embody the Sewell worldview are given training
opportunities in a stunning retreat setting. There is low
tolerance for cultural violations—and zero tolerance for
anything that hints at a lapse in ethics.

At the end of the year, all employees are celebrated
at a lavish annual party, where they get to experience the
type of impeccable service Sewell aspires to deliver in
the world. The highlight of this event? When CEO Carl
Sewell, son of the company's founder, takes the micro-
phone. And tells stories.

Consistency: Walk the Walk

One of our favorite management books that got far too little attention was *Management Lessons from Mayo Clinic*. It's a magnificent chronicle of how one of the best hospitals in the world
delivers excellence by putting patients first and innovating
around the still-revolutionary notion of team-based medicine.

The book also speaks to the leadership philosophy of former CEO Glenn Forbes. Forbes fiercely protected and grew the Mayo Clinic's culture of excellence. And he summed up the challenge this way: "If you've just communicated a value but you haven't driven it into the operations, into the policy, into the decision making, into the allocation of resources, and ultimately into the culture of the organization, then it's just words."[11]

As Forbes suggests, it's not enough to talk the talk on culture, although that's an important part of it. You have to make sure that the values you talk about inform the actions you take, in every part of the organization. And you have to stay on the lookout for gaps between words and deeds. At the Mayo Clinic, the staff has a well-worn phrase that's tossed out whenever the threat of a cultural break creeps into a decision: "Is this right for the patients or not?" The question sobers up meetings and brings everyone back to the organization's central purpose.[12] Similarly, as Sewell Automotive faced its own growing pains and joys, every decision point was considered in the context of culture. An ongoing and explicit discussion in the Sewell boardroom was whether a move reinforced or undermined its culture of honesty, integrity, hard work, and service.

Zappos—no surprise here—also makes sure that its culture of happiness permeates everything, including the minutiae of call center policy. In most call centers, employees are pressured to limit their customer interactions to three minutes. At Zappos, there's no limit and employees are encouraged to improvise. Zappos call center employees can even recite their personal record, which refers to the longest call they've ever had with a customer. In early 2011, the highest personal record we had heard about was over eight hours long.

"We don't use scripts," CEO Hsieh told us. "If you call one time, you might get a rep who is chatty or telling jokes, but another time, it might be someone who hears a dog barking in the background and develops a personal emotional connection that way. Or maybe you're from the same hometown. We don't care, as long as the customer walks away wowed by the experience."

But making people happy doesn't mean lowering standards (a common misperception), which would also be a cultural violation at Zappos. The company has high expectations of its people, and so it routinely churns out the bottom-performing 10 percent of employees each year. "You have to be willing to fire those to stay committed to the culture," says Hsieh.

If you haven't driven change at Zappos, you'll be held back. That's why you lose points if there are no mistakes noted on your review. You're being too conservative. Call center employees are rated on attendance and punctuality, but 50 percent of their review is based on "contribution to culture and core values." And not unlike Commerce Bank, Zappos has an unstructured peer recognition program. A certain number of "Zollars" are allocated to each department, which the teams can then award to members who have made specific contributions to core values. These are redeemable at the company "Zollar" store.

Zappos's professional development program is called Pipeline. According to Roger Dana, head of training communication and process development, it's built on the assumption that anyone can reach the highest level of management. To help, there is a full-time career coach on staff, with a two- to three-week waiting list for a thirty-minute appointment.

When we asked Hsieh, "Why isn't everyone doing what you do?" he answered, "Because there's not an immediate payoff. I'm taking a long-term view of the organization."

"In thirty years, we may have a Zappos airline," he says, only half joking.

Decalcify Your Company

Alignment isn't just a challenge across functions and levels—reinforcing and sustaining a culture of excellence is also a challenge over time. Culture, like other things, can dry out and harden with age. One reason is repetitive exposure to similar situations, and the kind of shorthand thinking that takes place as a result. Psychologists use the term *heuristics* to refer to the prepackaged responses that our minds use to make quick decisions, thereby failing to see the nuances.

A terrific article in *Harvard Business Review* described a scenario in which a car company received letters of complaint from disgruntled customers.[a] One of these unhappy drivers was a woman who kept bringing her car back for vague and unresolvable problems. Eventually, the company replaced the car for her, and she still kept coming back with the same sorts of problems. The employees had her pegged as the customer from hell. They became ever more dismissive of her complaints and disparaging of her personally. What's amazing is that when we use this case in a teaching setting, the same things start to happen. Students quickly begin to size up the woman in the same condescending way. "Some people are just never satisfied." "She must be a nutcase." But the moral of the story is that the woman's complaints were perfectly valid. She was not the customer from hell, but had instead been sold the cars from hell. Imagine yourself in this woman's position—dealing with all that wasted time and money and being treated as if you were crazy.

When they are in constant contact with customers, employees often get a disproportionate exposure to the bad. When things are going great, customers rarely call their car company or cell phone provider to let it know. And what this disproportionate exposure to the bad means is that *calcification* often sets in. Employees become hardened toward customers and start treating them as two-dimensional entities. But it's impossible to deliver excellent service when you've dehumanized your customer. So cultures not only have to get the norms and values right, but also have to provide for what we call regular *decalcification.* How much decalcification you're going to need will depend on how much hardening has occurred.

We recently taught this lesson at Kaiser Permanente, a leading health-care organization that recounted that at some of its really difficult call center positions, where staff spends the entire day being bombarded by complaints, employees have to be decalcified *every four hours.* Given the type of problems and stories you're being hit with, the high level of emotion associated with any sort of breakdown in the delivery of health services, you just can't help toughening up and closing yourself off to the person on the other line. And Kaiser Permanente discovered that the shutdown starts around hour four.

When does it set in at your organization?

a. Dan Ariely, "The Customers' Revenge," *Harvard Business Review,* December 2007, 31–43.

Putting It into Practice

Most companies internalize the culture-performance link the hard way—by allowing the development of a culture that undermines its performance goals. If you're lucky, you learn the lesson quickly, the way Verizon did in chapter 3, when, among other changes, it replaced a culture of execution with a culture of learning at its DSL call centers. We try to simulate this process for our own clients. Most companies have at least some aspect of their culture that they'd like to change, even if it's not yet standing in the way of progress. So rather than begin with a dauntingly blank slate and ask people to envision the ideal culture to support their performance goals (although this is one way to do it), we typically use Schein's culture framework (recall artifacts, behaviors, and shared assumptions) to help people diagnose what's happening right now in their existing cultures.

In most organizations, it's behaviors we want to change, and so the questions that matter are these:

- What's the problematic behavior?

- What are the shared basic assumptions driving that behavior?

- What can we do to change those assumptions?

Just wrestling with these questions can be empowering, since most people—even the most senior of managers—feel that their organizational culture is something they must endure, not something that is within their power to change.

For example, in one consulting firm we worked with, the problematic behavior was a lack of rigor in client analytics, a lack of intellectual curiosity around discovering and addressing the client's real issues. Everyone agreed right away on what needed to change. It took us a bit longer to surface the assumptions driving the behavior, but we could still measure the process in minutes. The central driving assumption, it turned out, was that performance ability and front-of-the-room skills were more valuable than getting to the truth. And the experience of employees kept bearing that out, since internal status gravitated toward the team's best communicators and performance artists. Close enough had become good enough, as long as presentations were delivered with confidence and flair. As a result, innovation at the firm stagnated and client satisfaction dropped. But these guys could definitely put on a good show.

The firm's partners concluded that they needed to credibly reorder the company's unspoken priorities. That would require a communications campaign and a change to both formal and informal incentives, including status cues. It would also require some soul-searching about whom they were hiring and promoting and about the behaviors the partners were modeling as leaders of the organization. Among other things, the firm's founder, a magnificent communicator and fundamentally an introvert, decided to open up his own analytic process and bring junior people around for the less glamorous work of cleaning and crunching data.

The next generation had only ever seen the founder give carefully crafted presentations, which he'd perfected privately and then delivered to wild applause. He'd historically done the prep work at home, at four in the morning, when no one else was awake to distract him. Now he decided to do at least some of it in the office. These sessions became informal tutorials for young staffers, opportunities to test and refine their client hypotheses, and a chance for the founder to find out what his people were learning out in the field. The organization caught on quickly.

In most cases, the culprit is good people behaving badly, not bad people behaving badly. If it's the latter, no cultural shift is going to help, by the way. Toxic or ineffective people simply need to be extracted, in part because of the cultural damage they will do. Keeping them around is an implicit endorsement of their behavior. But if you've got a team of good people and you know what kind of culture they need to deliver your version of excellence, now the fun starts: how exactly are you going to build it?

UNCOMMON TAKEAWAYS

✓ It's not enough to design your service model right. Uncommon service is achieved when great organizational design meets a culture of service excellence. A basic way to think about it is this: service excellence is a product of design and culture.

✓ The right culture is not a universal concept. Your right culture is a distinct asset that must be consistent with your organization's service model.

✓ One way to understand culture is to break it down into its relevant components. We like Edgar Schein's culture framework, which loosely divides a culture into artifacts, behaviors, and shared basic assumptions. As Schein argues, to change behavior (a company's typical goal), you have to change the way people think. To change the way people think, start with the underlying assumptions that drive that thinking.

✓ Great service organizations tend to do three things well in their relationship with culture. They have deep *clarity* about the organizational culture they must cultivate in order to compete and win. They are effective in *signaling* the norms and values that embody that culture. And they work hard to ensure cultural *consistency,* alignment between the desired culture and organizational strategy, structure, and operations.

Chapter Six

Getting Bigger

You've mastered the service excellence equation. You've made the hard trade-offs, and your well-behaved customers are happy. You've built a good team to deliver great value, within a culture that fuels your service advantage. At this point, most organizations start to get restless. They want to grow.

One reason is to keep it interesting. Shareholder pressure is another, perhaps the most urgent, but there is also the simple desire to create opportunity for your people. This aspiration surfaces regularly among managers of successful service companies. The people who helped you build your company are craving challenge and a sense of achievement, and growth can reliably deliver both.

Generally speaking, a company can grow in two ways. The first is to do more of what you're already doing (or closely related to it). The second is to do different things.[1] In the language of this book, doing more of what you're already doing is growing the existing service model. Doing different things means building new service models.

Let's start with the first challenge: scaling the model you've already got.

The Same Thing, Only Bigger

Most companies don't pause to think systematically about growth, particularly in the early stages of their life cycle. They don't have that luxury. Here's a common pattern: You're new. You're scrappy. You'll do whatever it takes to meet the needs of your clients, which means growth by any means necessary. If a customer wants to give your standard offering a slightly different spin, sure, you'll give it a try. Your effort is also known as customizing your product or service. At this point, there's such a premium on developing customer relationships that you're not thinking about how to pull this off in a profitable way. Instead, you're thinking about survival. If you can keep a growing number of customers happy, then good things are more likely to happen.

Eventually, you graduate from this opportunistic approach and start asking yourself some sobering questions. Which customers should I indulge, and which should I ignore? How do I get more operational control? What's my ultimate goal here (change the world? a nice retirement? an IPO?)?

When these kinds of questions start to haunt you, it's typically a good sign. It signals a pivot from the kind of customization we just described to some level of standardization. The trigger for this switch is usually the realization that it's not sustainable to keep delivering one-of-a-kind, made-to-order service. Your margins can't take it anymore. Moreover, the complexity of maintaining a wide range of distinct offerings makes the business difficult to scale operationally.

No one likes this moment. The word *standardization* sounds cold. It smacks of ignoring your customers' humanity, leaving their needs festering and unmet in exchange for a few more dollars in your investors' gilded pockets. Surely, the quality of your service will be sacrificed on the altar of greater efficiency.

One of our central messages in this chapter is that defying this trade-off is possible. In fact, it's not only possible, but also likely to be the only choice you have if you want to deliver excellence *and* grow. Remember the Hotel Cipriani? At the Cipriani, every service dimension is off the charts, and every nuance of the experience is unique to this particular establishment. As one of the Orient Express Hotels (OEH), the Cipriani belongs to the same corporate family as that of the equally exquisite Hotel Splendido in Portofino, but a stay in one of these hotels won't feel like a stay in the other, because each draws on the traditions, cuisines, and talents of its immediate environment.

It takes a lifetime to master such customized perfection, and so OEH personnel are not transferred from one hotel to another. The Cipriani chef cooks not merely northern Italian but also Venetian cuisine and has been lord of the Cipriani kitchen since 1970. The hotel's general manager has been in her position of leadership since 1977. Longevity of service, tied to a profound sense of place, helps deliver the exceptional experience that, alas, costs much more than the next-best hotel in town.

But beyond the high cost to the consumer, the other major limitation of the OEH model is that it is not an engine of growth. In a plot of customization versus quality, OEH lives in the upper right quadrant, representing high quality and high customization (figure 6–1). The Four Seasons, a competing

FIGURE 6-1

The quality-customization matrix of service

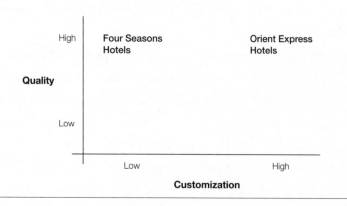

FIGURE 6-1

The quality-customization matrix of service

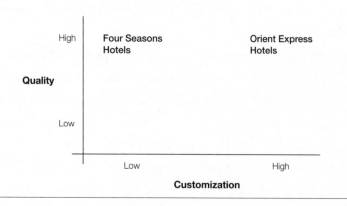

luxury hotel brand, lives in the upper left: high quality and high standardization (i.e., low customization). The distinction of interest here is that the Four Seasons—which delivers reliably excellent service—is perfectly structured for growth.

The low customization of the Four Seasons service model allows it to scale at a healthy clip. And here's the beautiful thing: loyal patrons of the Cipriani would hardly feel out of place at a Four Seasons. Checking into a Four Seasons property, they'd enjoy a comparable level of attentiveness as they immersed themselves in the luxurious feel of an exclusive experience. No service they consumed on-site would feel standardized in any way that made it less than desirable. But visit a dozen Four Seasons, and check out the water glasses, or compare the doorman's greeting and uniform in Boston and San Francisco. A highly refined consistency is the secret to the brand's success.

It's entirely possible to deliver excellence from a highly standardized platform. So how do you get there?

Saying No to Grandma

Most customized processes accrete over time, usually inadvertently—the natural evolution we noted a moment ago. A customer wants something, and there's no good reason—at least no reason that feels compelling enough—not to accommodate the request at the time. And then this flexibility gets institutionalized. A valuable first step in the standardization process, therefore, is to revisit these legacy decisions. Which of your customized processes are no longer defensible? Where are you giving up more than you're getting by saying yes to certain demands?

A favorite anecdote circulated among business school faculty is about Herb Kelleher, founder of Southwest Airlines, and the clarity with which he once responded to a customer complaint about Southwest's policy of not transferring bags to other airlines.[2] Apparently, the complaint letter systematically outlined the many hardships that a brittle-boned grandmother had to endure while trying to fly cross-country to see her grandchildren, and how much easier her life would be if Southwest would do her the simple courtesy of transferring her luggage, a service that all other airlines had kindly figured out how to offer. Kelleher responded in the same point-by-point manner of the letter, pointing out that Southwest's business model, which delivered lower prices on the backs of faster turnaround times, wouldn't survive making an exception like this. Herb felt her pain, but no, he wouldn't take care of her bags.

We like this story because we think of our own grandmothers and how hard it would have been to say no to them. It's become an iconic image in our minds, saying no to grandma, but in return, you get to build the most successful airline in the world.

A major driver of increasing customization is simply listening to, and trying to please, your customers. Of course, the answer is not to ignore them. It's to listen to them strategically and to customize where it counts. Customize where you can deliver real value and get paid for it without wreaking havoc on your operations—but not where you make a few customers happy at the expense of large swaths of employees, stockholders, and other customers.

One way to get the balance right is point-of-sale customization (right at the very end) backed up by a highly standardized operation. In other words, the customer gets to tweak a few relatively minor things that can be easily managed by frontline workers. But the back-office looks and acts the same, regardless of what they order. This structure tends to scale gracefully, while driving high levels of satisfaction. Think Burger King's "Have it your way!" slogan, which does not at all mean you can have it your way. It means, "We'll hold the pickles and onions if you ask us, but it doesn't mean we'll grill up a veggie Whopper or anything else that's not on the menu." This is what is typically meant by the phrase *mass customization.*

The Tex-Mex phenomenon Chipotle does mass customization well with a very limited menu that customers can mix and match however they'd like. The restaurant chain lets you do anything you want with a narrow selection of beans, rice, meat, veggies, salsa, and tortillas. Most customers just throw in the towel and order a burrito, but it's *their* burrito, with precisely the right amount of salsa they dictate to the responsive staff working on the fresh, beautiful, customer-facing assembly line. By any measure of performance, Chipotle is hitting it out of the park. In 2010, the company was serving customers from more than a thousand locations in thirty-eight states, collecting almost $2 billion in revenues.

Lululemon is a successful apparel company that focuses on the burgeoning yoga market. It recently expanded from indoor clothing to rain jackets. Why? Customer demand, head of marketing, Eric Petersen, told the *New York Times:* "They asked for it."[3] We're confident that the company's back-end decision process was much more strategic than that, but the comment stood out to us as being too close to the way too many service companies make decisions about growth. Our point here is to not run your business by the comment box. It may feel good, at least at first, but here's the catch: customers typically don't understand the implications of their requests. It's your obligation—to them and to you—to put their demands in context, to evaluate the trade-offs of expanding your offering.

CASE STUDY

The Growth "Flywheel" at Rackspace

In ten years, San Antonio–based Rackspace, a global leader in the hosting and cloud computing industry, grew from $12 million in revenue to $800 million, and from one hundred employees to four thousand. Its growth has been nothing short of meteoric.[a]

What's the lesson? Rackspace first had to get its service model under control before it had any chance of expansion. The company started by retooling its service offering, a series of trade-offs it stumbled on when it ran out of money with its first strategy. The lack of resources—an event CEO Lanham Napier describes as a "blessing"—forced the company to confront the brutal truth that its original service model wasn't working. That model was designed to rent out server hardware and then basically to wish customers the best in figuring out how to use it. Cofounders Pat Condon and Dirk Elmendorf characterized the original concept: "If you don't know how to use the technology . . . that's your problem." Since conventional wisdom had convinced the team that meaningful customer support wasn't affordable or scalable, very little resources were being directed toward it.

The combination of an empty bank account and a pattern of angry service calls led to a breakthrough that defied the industry's prevailing assumptions: Rackspace's best shot would be to viably deliver a premium offering the company characterized as "fanatical service." So the company began to build a service model and service culture to pull it off:

- *Key trade-off in its offering:* Higher prices would be needed in exchange for a high-touch, high-service experience.

- *Funding mechanism:* In addition to higher prices, the real key would be higher retention. By the company's estimates, existing, satisfied customers were up to ten times more profitable than new customers. As a result, according to CEO Napier, the company funds its premium service levels through customer retention: "We don't see service as a cost, we see it as an investment."

- *Employee management system:* The company uses values-based selection of "rackers"; clear, team-based incentives; and lots of decision rights in the hands of the front line—"not the guy in the finance office," according to Napier, who recognizes that it's a "frightening concept . . . but you have to believe that over time, [frontline employees] will make the right decision."

- *Customer management:* Rigorous tracking tools—a pricing tool, a churn tool, a retention tool—make the profitability of every customer completely transparent, along with the cost of every internal action. Employees use these tools to develop deep intuition about customer behavior and nudge customers into the bounds of expected profitability.

And then there's the Rackspace culture. Its distinction is codified in a series of living values that starts with "fanatical support." Focusing on service as a mission for the slightly unhinged encourages people to bring their humanity into the workplace, even the crazy parts, which helps them to connect with customers in an authentic way.

Rackspace's most remarkable assumption, which informs almost every decision the company makes, is the belief in the capability of the workforce. Napier calls his employees "precious entities." They're treated that way, not with kid gloves or lavish rewards (although clear recognition, monetary and otherwise, is part of it), but with a celebration of their unique gifts and quirks. Sometimes that means a customized management approach that's designed to enable an individual's strengths. And sometimes that means renting out a movie theater so the company can go see *Transformers* together. "We're a bunch of geeks," Napier clarifies, by way of explanation.

The CEO is animated in discussing all aspects of the Rackspace business model, but never more so than when he talks about his employees: "I'll look you straight in the eye and tell you that I think they're the best humanity has to offer." Rackers have internalized Napier's belief, which gives them permission to deliver uncommon service to both their customers and each other.

It all adds up to a virtuous cycle of growth. The team's assumption is simple: if they serve customers well, customers will give them more work. It means that Rackspace will grow 20 percent in any given year without adding a single new customer. Napier describes it as a flywheel that starts with happy employees delivering excellent service. Excellent service leads to stronger, more successful client businesses, which leads to increased demand for Rackspace services. That increased demand is more profitable to service, since Rackspace has already learned exactly how to satisfy it. And the cycle begins again. It's what our colleagues Earl Sasser, Jim Heskett, and Len Schlesinger call the "service profit chain," and it's alive and well at Rackspace.[b]

Napier's flywheel keeps accelerating. Eight years into its growth sprint, Rackspace is growing faster than at any period in the company's history, despite its larger size. As Napier himself pointed out, "that's crazy."

a. Information presented in this case is derived from W. Earl Sasser, Jr., James L. Heskett, and Tom Ryder, "Rackspace Hosting (2000)," video, product number 9–811-701 (Boston: Harvard Business School, 2010).

b. James L. Heskett, W. Earl Sasser Jr., and Leonard A. Schlesinger, *The Service Profit Chain* (New York: Free Press, 1997).

Customers aren't the only source of customization chaos. One reason a telecom company we studied received 8 million calls each month (out of 12 million customers) was that it was inhabiting the lower right quadrant of the quality-customization matrix in figure 6–1, producing highly customized, low-quality service. The company was customizing all kinds of processes, but it wasn't making the customer better off.

How did it get there? The company had grown through acquisitions, and as each of those deals was being finalized, it had seemed a painless sweetener to let each regional group maintain its own systems and procedures. This led to offerings that were produced, billed, and managed through an incredibly diverse mix of inconsistent processes. It meant that while a smaller competitor with a standardized system could quickly roll out an innovation, this company took the competitive equivalent of forever to do something similar. And the chaos and mistakes ensured that its customers were reliably unhappy.

A Brief Aside on Getting Bigger *and* Better

In our experience, a shared characteristic of successful, fast-growing companies is a relentless curiosity about what's *not* working. These companies aren't politically conflicted about how to acknowledge or discuss problems. They welcome them, openly, as opportunities.

Again, Toyota was among the most visible organizations to celebrate this mentality, until it lost its way (hopefully, briefly) when it shifted its focus to growth rather than improvement. When new managers at Toyota got hired, their first assignment was to stand in a box outlined on the floor with red tape, facing the assembly line. The recruits weren't allowed to leave that box until they saw something that could be improved in the process. Keep in mind that this was the celebrated Toyota production system, perfected over more than a decade, and so some new hires spent their entire first week on the job just standing in that red box. Others spent less than an hour. Either way, it was seared into their souls that their responsibility as an employee was to make the place better.

How do you treat people who identify problems in your organization? How have you been treated as the squeaky wheel? "Don't bring me a problem unless you bring me a solution" is among the most dangerous phrases in the American management playbook. It's a recipe for sluggish growth and unrealized potential. In fact, one diagnostic we've developed for sizing up a company's growth prospects is whether the CEO makes it clear nonverbally that he or she welcomes bad news. We've found it startlingly reliable.

If you're preparing for significant growth, we recommend paying loving attention to even the small problems. Most organizations have an implicit 80-20 rule, a belief that 20 percent of the problems are causing 80 percent of the harm. The built-in assumption is that if you can resolve the big ones, you'll be OK. But an HBS colleague, Anita Tucker, has found that it's the small problems that often cripple companies. Small problems often don't get addressed, because they don't seem significant enough to warrant focus. But because they don't get addressed, they always require a work-around, and that work-around can consume 20 percent of an employee's day. People can spend 20 percent of their time on the job working around problems that will never make it onto the priority list to be fixed.

Tucker conducted a study of a nursing unit and found that on average, each employee wasted one hour per day working around problems that could be fixed, but that no one deemed important enough to address.[a] An hour every *day*. What could your company achieve if it gave an extra five hours a week to every employee?

a. A. L. Tucker, "An Empirical Study of System Improvement by Frontline Employees in Hospital Units," *Manufacturing and Service Operations Management* 9, no. 4 (fall 2007): 492–505.

The Multifocused Firm

There's an alternative to scaling a standardized version of your existing service model: build multiple models within the same organizational structure. If you find that your current strategy is attracting scrappy, more focused competitors, while delivering mediocre margins and high levels of complexity, you may be a good candidate for this approach. But it's not emotionally easy to reach this conclusion. Here's how the story typically plays out.

For the best of reasons and with admiral intentions, you've begun to satisfy a greater variety of needs for a greater variety of customers. This direction has become broad and unwieldy, straining to accommodate wide-ranging customer demands with all their attendant operational complexity. Some of your customers have come to you because of price, some because of location, and some simply because of a merger, and quite possibly against their will. To keep up with them all, you've hired a wide range of employees to deliver a wide range of offerings. Like a cargo ship, you've become heavy and slow.

Enter the upstart competitor—in a speedboat. It turns out that each operating segment you've managed to attract could sustain a separate, tightly focused service model. And so the new entrant shows up to pick off one of those segments with a narrow product set and a narrow set of employees.[4]

Five Stages of Strategic Grief

How do you respond to a new entrant? In our experience, the reaction often unfolds in stages that roughly mirror the famous five stages of grief.[5]

Stage 1: Denial

If you could bug the executive offices at a large company confronting a focused entrant, you'd hear a chorus of dismissive managers. Focused entrants tend to be small and shamelessly inadequate on certain dimensions—they have nothing to lose by daring to be bad—but this makes it easy to not take them seriously at first. Commerce Bank? Their rates are pathetic! Southwest Airlines? They don't even feed you! Boarding their planes is like a riot at a bus station! By focusing on their "weaknesses," you feel better. Until . . .

Stage 2: Anger

Denial is soon replaced by anger, ushered in by the realization that profitable customers have abandoned you to do business with the unworthy competitor. There was one clear pattern in the Citibank customers who crossed the street to get to Commerce Bank—they were all willing to trade good rates for excellent service. In other words, they were not price-sensitive, and customers who are not price-sensitive tend to be profitable. This is a classic challenge for an industry's reigning player. Your best customers are often the first to jump.

Stage 3: Rationalization

Stage 3 is where the competitive brain can become the most delusional. In this stage, you'll often do anything to diminish the seriousness of the threat, in your own mind and the minds of your stakeholders. "Fine," you'll say. "The new guy has stolen some of our customers, but not all of them. We're still reaching everyone else." Here companies often bring in outside consultants to validate their worldview. So what if you're being beaten in one small market, right? *Right?*

Stage 4: Despair

At this stage, you give into your feelings of dread. Let's stay with our retail banking example. Once you stop deluding yourself, reality is not pleasant to confront. It's not just Commerce Bank that's popped up on your horizon. Commerce has entered the game on the basis of its hours and attitude, but then along comes ING Direct, which is equally optimized but on very different performance features. ING Direct has very few branches and the worst physical access in the world, but it offers the very best interest rates on savings.

Especially in previously regulated industries, it often takes a while for new entrants to get a foothold. But eventually it becomes clear that these competitors are not going away. The time between no new players and one new player may be several years, but then the span between one new player and two new players is shorter, and between two and three is shorter still. Stage 4 often kicks in here, when it's a pileup of new entrants. This presents a very good reason to feel bad.

Stage 5: Acceptance

At this stage, managers make peace with the truth and begin to deal with it strategically. The faster you get to this stage, the better, and we see it as our job to speed up this process. At whatever stage we find companies, we view it as an obligation to try to propel them to stage 5.

Portfolios of Services

In our work with companies that successfully withstand the onslaught of focused competitors, we've found that most organizations aren't terribly resilient in the face of the challenge. When a focused competitor comes into an industry, incumbents tend to suffer. And they often respond with a buying spree. Acquisitions mask many sins. You feel better because you're bigger, but it often means your company is weaker. That strategy only lasts so long.

But every once in a while, there's an incumbent that prevails on its own merits. One pattern among successful defenders is that they tend to fit the profile of what we call a *multi-focused firm*. This means that they've built multiple service models—business units or brands, depending on the structure of the organization—that are each individually optimized for a distinct operating segment, each strategically good and bad at certain things. In other words, each of these companies has a *portfolio* of the kind of well-designed service models we've described throughout the book. Rather than expand their existing service models to do more, these organizations added new service models beneath the same corporate umbrella.

For example, when Best Buy expanded into high-end electronics, it launched Magnolia, a store within a store, which is actually a service model within a service model. Best Buy's core customer is a price-sensitive, do-it-yourself electronics consumer who will spring for products priced from $50 to a few thousand dollars, at most. Magnolia sells ultra-luxury home entertainment systems and other audiovisual "artistry" that promises, literally, to "transform the way you live." The

Magnolia team will sell you the best of the best, while also turning a spare bedroom into an automated, surround-sound theater experience that can compete with the multiplex down the street.

Magnolia plays a very important role in the Best Buy strategy—it allows the company to grow without confusing or repelling its target demographic. Armani used a similar strategy when it created Armani Exchange (A/X). Giorgio Armani Boutiques carry a high-end, ready-to-wear line that only a tiny fraction of the world's consumers can afford. These shops even dabble in elements of couture, offering customized shirts and suits made to the exact specifications of brand acolytes. A/X, in contrast, brings the designer's unique vision to the people, or at least to more of the people, those with caps on their discretionary income but with a deep appreciation for fashion. But the inventory at A/X is not a diluted version of what's being sold in the boutiques. The A/X offering is younger, edgier, more rock and roll. Whereas the boutique offers exquisite service from salespeople who double as personal shoppers, the A/X service model is geared toward an empowered Gen Y consumer who knows what he or she wants and distrusts the meddling of a profit-motivated stranger. Armani shoppers are coddled; A/X customers are lovingly ignored.

The point of these examples is that consumers are interacting with two companies but four very different service models. It's perhaps most vivid in Magnolia versus Best Buy, since they often share the same real estate. Best Buy hits you, bright and shiny, like a flea market for things with plugs—in-your-face salespeople, unforgiving lights, and row after row of electronic goods. Cross the threshold into the Magnolia section of the store, and things immediately feel very different. It's quiet and serene. The lighting is dim. Only a few choice items are on display, next to comfortable chairs that encourage you to sit down and inhale the possibility.

Shared Services

Here's the trick for incumbents: the experiences we just described *feel* very different to consumers, but they share lots of back-end processes. The Best Buys and Armanis of the world can compete with players that are more focused, because the two companies gain certain advantages by linking multiple models together. In other words, each service model in the company somehow makes the other service model better off. In Best Buy's case, for example, two distinct models share one location (a very tricky thing to pull off), which achieves economies of scale on real estate.

We call this structure *shared services.* It's also how the hugely successful health-care advertising agency Cline Davis & Mann (CDM) took its growth to the next level.

Substance, Style, Conviction, and Grace: Collaboration at the CDM Group

CDM had hardly languished at any time since it launched in New York in 1984. In 1997, when it became part of Omnicom, the agency had 141 people and about $30 million in revenue. Within the next ten years, the agency grew to 876 people and revenues increased more than sixfold.[6]

During that time, CDM's formula for growth was "as much about retaining top talent as it was about capturing the market opportunity," says Ed Wise, chairman and CEO of the

CDM Group. "The perennial challenge in the agency world is that the best talent always rises at a very rapid pace. If you ask those people what their dream is, you usually get the same answer: 'Someday I'd like to run my own agency.'"

CDM embraced that answer and decided to grow by spinning off smaller boutique agencies within the larger company and then putting its best people in charge. CDM Princeton was one example, a three-person effort to make the most of a relationship with a single client in a single geographical area. A year later, CDM rolled out CDMiConnect, an interactive and relationship marketing group, as another three-person stand-alone entity. According to Carol DiSanto, now president of the CDM Group, "that breeding of agencies has produced what many consider to be the most complete portfolio of health-care marketing practices in the world."

In 2006, the complexity of managing the infrastructure of all its businesses—facilities, finance, human resources, and IT—forced CDM to rethink its approach. Up until this point, oversight of these functions had been left to the agency leaders, which led to high variability in performance, duplication of effort, and underutilization of resources. Operations management was also rarely the passion of the client-facing executives who once dreamed of starting their own agencies.

So CDM tried something new. The first step was to recruit C-level executives, for example, a chief financial officer, a chief human resources officer, and a chief information officer, to oversee internal service functions. Each of them reported to CDM New York, and their mission was to figure out how to leverage the resources of each CDM business for the benefit of all CDM businesses.

The next step was the hard one—pulling the back-office business of running the agencies out of the individual shops and giving these new chiefs full authority to manage it. In effect, business development, facilities, finance, education, and IT would become their shared-services mandate, and the individual agencies would become their clients. Beginning in 2008, anybody working in any of these groups was no longer employed by an individual agency. Instead the employee reported to his or her functional chiefs.

Agencies would retain full decision rights over anything related to their own clients: creative, accounting, strategic, medical, and scientific affairs. Trying to centralize any of these activities, CDM reasoned, would defeat the purpose. The minute that happened, the strength and effectiveness of the individual brands would begin to erode.

The company also wanted to avoid the appearance of adding a layer of management with higher status than the people who led the client work. But this required a careful balance. CDM was painfully aware that shared-services initiatives often fail because the leaders of the back-office service units don't have the status or leadership ability to drive uncomfortable, but necessary change throughout the organization. The company also understood that these new operations managers had to be unambiguously great at their jobs—they had to be of a caliber that none of the individual business units could have afforded to hire on their own.

According to DiSanto, the managers immediately justified their existence by identifying lots of low-hanging fruit, in terms of both cost savings and identifying additional opportunities: "The benefits of [these opportunities] would be impossible for us to capture unless we enforced a greater level of centralization across our businesses."

One simple example was e-mail, where all CDM businesses realized cost savings, improved performance, and greater maintenance efficiency by bringing everyone on to a common platform. But as the opportunities became more complex, the shared-services managers were able to clearly demonstrate the value of change. In finance, for example, the new CFO brought in a range of new tools to manage profitability across the organization. One of these was a way to monitor utilization, which had the immediate impact of raising total utilization in key departments from an average of 76 percent to over 85 percent in less than six months.

CDM's shared-services initiative succeeded where many other organizations have failed. What made the difference for CDM, we believe, was its focus on better performance, not just lower costs. Internal resistance to CDM's efforts bubbled up initially, but faded when the agency heads also began to see it this way. Rather than focusing on a loss of control, they began to see the restructuring as liberating. Soon these directors were asking the same questions that animated the New York team: What can you take off my plate so that I can make my own clients better off? It turns out no one really missed overseeing health insurance plans and the nuances of building security.

Citing CDM's commitment to bring in great talent and then give these people room to sprint, DiSanto is convinced that the shared-services model is consistent with that core belief: "In centralizing a set of functional areas, we could attract talent that our individual businesses were not able to afford and can leverage their skills to the benefit of our entire network." Moreover, each unit could also benefit from the recruiting efforts of others. This is particularly important in the area of temporary workers—contingent resources—which can represent a huge expenditure. These are the people who audit or reset retail displays, serve as brand ambassadors at retail locations, or distribute samples at events.

Now at the same time that CDM's service quality improved, costs also went down. Creating a shared, high-performance back office allowed for things like reductions in head count, rolling out standardized technology solutions, and collectively negotiating fees with headhunters. But lowering costs was not the central focus of these efforts—CDM's mission was to reduce the complexity of agency operations and thereby increase the value it was delivering to its clients.

It created a separate holding company to get there, which is not the only structural option. CDM initially went looking for an "un-brand" for this new organization. It didn't want each agency to be a clone, but it did want there to be something consistent at the core. The values the company cherished most were substance, style, conviction, and grace. Thus, the name of the shared-services group—the core that everyone would share—became SSCG. The holding company eventually changed its name to the CDM Group, both to build on the equity of the CDM name and to expand its strategic options (and because explaining all those letters became a distraction). But the idea stayed alive—a network held together by a shared set of values.

For the first year, the costs of the CDM Group, except for its directors' compensation, were allocated on a monthly basis to the profit-and-loss statements of each individual agency, according to its percentage of total headcount. This was not a casual design choice; nor were the choices that followed. According to CEO Wise, "to assess what else might make sense, we considered functions where all our 'parts' could profit from the scale of 'the whole.'" And so CDM soon discovered yet another way to think about shared services: a mechanism for sharing insight and learning across agencies. We call this realizing *economies of experience*. CDM looked to its own holding company, Omnicom, to help it pull off this strategy of economies of experience. And that's when things really got interesting.

Economies of Experience

Omnicom has developed a centralized strategy for unleashing the knowledge that was getting locked up in individual managers and companies. The highest-performing people in the Omnicom network are nominated to attend a one-week executive training program. Often held on remote college campuses, the training sessions are intense, running from early morning until late into the night.

As a taste of how serious Omnicom is about pursuing economies of experience, students at "Omnicom University" are given a research project to complete on their own time during the subsequent year. If they carry out their assignment as agreed, they return for a second week-long session twelve months later. The research assignments are turned in, approved, and then fleshed out by two professional case writers known as the "two Dans." Dan Maher and Dan O'Brien, the best team we've seen in collaborating to bring case studies to life, are a vital part of knowledge sharing at Omnicom. Their cases then become the basis for the following year's curriculum. Faculty from top business schools are recruited to deliver the content, and the takeaways are lessons specifically grounded in the Omnicom universe. Leading the charge is former vice chairman of Omnicom, Tom Watson, who is also the founding dean of Omnicom University.

The model has inspired the CDM Group as its own strategy and business model have evolved. The CDM Group is increasingly playing a role in delivering collaborative teams across service models. With guidance from the centralized holding company, an average client now engages three to five CDM brands. So not only is the CDM Group leveraging economies of scale and experience for its own agencies, but it's also helping clients to benefit more directly from these advantages. Wise's view of the future, in fact, is now one where CDM agencies are "fiercely collaborative" with each other. He sees the iPhone as a useful metaphor: "We need an elegant interface that allows our customers to have an extraordinary user experience with seamless access to our full breadth of capabilities. So we are not just a bunch of silos glued together. But instead we are something better, synergistic and efficient." He believes that this vision is a natural extension of the initial reorganization around shared services.

Realizing economies of experience across CDM brands is now the focus of Wise's efforts. To get there, he has put together a central learning and training team that pulls from the senior ranks of each agency. Called the Collaboration Project, the group is charged with learning from each other and then "mentoring" their own companies. Together, project team members have developed a coordination model that will be piloted throughout the CDM network in 2011.

Examples of this kind of centralized training model can be found elsewhere in the corporate universe. But in our experience, Omnicom and the CDM Group are both exceptional in the strength of their commitment to sharing knowledge across large networks. The only other model we've seen in this league is General Electric's legendary Crotonville, the company's center for corporate learning. Crotonville may go down in history as the only corporate training program to achieve enough visibility to be deliciously parodied on prime-time television, in this case by Tina Fey and the other writers of *30 Rock.*

Crotonville has earned its distinction. The model allowed GE to become a leader in achieving economies of scale and experience, including internal markets that introduce competition, accountability, and transparency. Jack Welch, the former (and increasingly iconic) CEO, believed in problem solving across units and across organizational layers, so the talent brought to Crotonville comes from all ranks. GE's approach to knowledge transfer explicitly leverages experience across service models, including formalized best-practice sharing, centralized employee training, and the rotation of managers among models. The prevailing philosophy at GE has always been that if an individual unit contributes value to the other units, then it stays within the GE portfolio. If a unit fails to contribute beyond its own boundaries, it's time to consider spinning it off.

The fast-food industry, in particular, seems to benefit from this approach. Yum Brands is a collection of five familiar brands: Pizza Hut, Taco Bell, KFC, Long John Silver, and A&W, all businesses that occupy space close to one another in the grand scheme of the restaurant world.

At one time, three of these brands, Pizza Hut, Taco Bell, and KFC, were all PepsiCo, Inc., companies, but they functioned with an opposite structure from what we mean by shared services. Not only was there really no mutual gain from the presence of the other brands, but they also competed with each other in unproductive ways. The executives presiding over each of these brands were pushing to visibly outdo the others so that they could step out of fast food (once considered a neglected stepchild at Pepsi) and into the mainstream of the beverage business. They even bid against each other for prime real estate, which ratcheted up the price for all three units. Performance was predictably mediocre, and the brands were eventually spun off as a group.

And that's when the shared-services story gets interesting. On the first day after the new company—Yum Brands—was constituted, CEO David Novak designed a model to ensure that as an organization, Yum Brands would use its three approaches to delivering good food to improve the presence of all three brands. Taco Bell, under Yum Brands, would be better than Taco Bell alone.

In terms of economies of scale, for example, Yum Brands quickly became one of the largest purchasers of cheese in the world. Its greatest economies of experience emerged from figuring out effective ways to deal with franchising. One of these techniques was to establish voluntary purchasing requirements. Other food chains owned by large parent companies insist on in-house purchasing, even when the business unit could get a better deal by driving down to Costco and loading up the minivan. At Yum Brands, franchisees can purchase through the company or go elsewhere. The fact that 95 percent rely on Yum Brands speaks to the quality and value of the shared services delivered by the company.

It's 6:00 Somewhere: Shared Services at Zappos

In 2006, Zappos noticed that current and past-season shoes would often appear side-by-side in customer searches. This was particularly true for running shoes, as the styles don't change that much from one season to the next. COO Alfred Lin told us, "We were featuring last year's running shoe alongside this year's, with last year's style priced at 20 percent less. This encouraged customers who would have been willing to buy this year's style at full price to buy last year's instead. We needed to separate our service-oriented from our value-oriented customer."

In 2007, Zappos announced it would acquire 6pm.com, an online outlet for discounted shoes, clothing, and accessories, and move the company's headquarters from Denver to Las Vegas. An integration plan was in place: 6pm.com would join the Zappos family, but keep a separate identity, customer base, and service model.

Nearly 90 percent of 6pm.com's brands were already available through Zappos.com. But this was no Zappos redux. The value-focused site offered merchandise at a 40 to 75 percent discount, charged customers for shipping, and supported customers largely by e-mail. Although 6pm.com provided lower-quality service than Zappos did, the service was still higher than what other discount outlets offered.

Why grow in this way? Zappos saw a few reasons to do it, including the chance to achieve real economies of experience. Employees at 6pm.com could get the same basic training that Zappos employees received, even though the discounter would enforce different terms and policies (e.g., returns were limited to 30 days instead of 365, shipping charges applied, and the call center maintained more limited hours, from Sunday to Friday, 9 a.m. to 5 p.m.). And the culture—the parent company's true advantage—would be pure Zappos. "Anyone who competes on price alone is not going to have loyalty for long if they aren't always the lowest," said CEO Tony Hsieh.

The structural synergy went beyond sharing back-office functions like training. Not only did 6pm.com give Zappos a way to reach value-conscious customers, but the discount company also gave Zappos a mechanism for moving discontinued and past-season merchandise—which then allowed Zappos to close all but one of its retail stores. Zappos discovered that in less than a month, 6pm.com could sell what all the Zappos outlet stores combined could sell in an entire year. With 6pm.com acting as a liquidation channel for Zappos, everybody walked away winning.

The 6pm.com acquisition was not the company's first experiment with building new service models on a foundation of shared services and assets. Zappos had already created new service models that leveraged its capacity for extraordinary service. In 2000, the company introduced Powered By Zappos (PBZ) a separate business-to-business unit that maintained Web sites for other companies. PBZ will warehouse a client's inventory, ship the products, and operate its call centers—which amounts to what one client called "end-to-end e-commerce services." Zappos called it being a "ghost writer for Web sites." In addition to leveraging its service strengths, PBZ helped to increase returns on the company's investment in its Kentucky warehouse, as well as gain larger economies of scale for its shipping operation. In 2009, Zappos was maintaining PBZ sites for manufacturers ranging from Clark's shoes to LEGO toys.

Zappos also found a way to achieve economies of experience outside the boundaries of its own business units. Zappos Insights is a members-only, online resource developed in 2009 in response to the flood of inquiries from other companies hoping to emulate its success. The site provides video interviews with senior managers, articles, and other resources to give its clients access to the inside story of Zappos's rocket-fueled growth. The fee for the subscription service is $39.95 per month.

Premium retail, value retail, IT services, executive training. At first blush—and to the wide range of end users—this jumble of industries and offerings seems incoherent. But to Zappos, it makes all the sense in the world.

To be clear, models like these are distinct from the conglomerate structure that arrived with a bang in the 1980s, only to flame out within the decade. The 1980s conglomerate was typically little more than a way for corporations to hedge their bets—to carry an umbrella while wearing sunscreen. These businesses were cobbled together, but derived little mutual benefit from being linked.

The shared-services models that are succeeding at CDM, Yum Brands, and Zappos bring separate brands under a common, corporate umbrella, but not just as a hedge against the failure of any one enterprise. In these models, distinct brands enhance each other—and enhance the service experience for their own customers. Again, the benefit comes primarily from economies of scale and experience that both reduce costs and improve quality.

The bundling we saw in the 1980s didn't deliver on the quality part of this equation. Conglomerates were created on the promise of cost savings, but these structures often sacrificed internal service units in the name of cost reduction, and quality typically plummeted. Making matters worse, they were often led by executives who demanded that business units rely on internal services providers, which hamstrung managers and gave the service groups no incentive to improve. The net result? Conglomerates often made their independent business units worse off than if the units had remained freestanding. This meant, as every corporate raider knew, that the aggregate was worth less than the sum of its parts.

Putting It into Practice

The incumbents who followed the shared-services model were so successful, and what they were doing seemed so sensible when we deconstructed it, that we couldn't figure out why so few companies had managed to pull it off. When we looked a bit closer, we found two organizational stumbling blocks that often chased away the shared-services dream: knowing where to draw the line and low-quality services.

Hard Lines

The first barrier to the shared-services model is the practical and political difficulty of answering the following questions: Where do you draw the line? Which resources and functions stay with the brand unit, and which can be aggregated at the corporate level under the mantle of shared services?

It's human nature to crave maximum control over your own destiny, and among brand managers on the rise, this desire is a powerful impulse. When these managers finally get their hands on a profit-and-loss statement, they want full accountability. They want complete control over costs and allocations—who gets hired, what the new hire gets paid, which systems are put in place, which vendors and consultants are engaged. The people in charge of these units often want the line drawn so that shared services are as tightly circumscribed as possible.

The people running shared services, of course, want the opposite. They, too, want to be accountable for the value they create, and a company can't pick up economies of scale unless everyone is playing along. You don't get bulk discounts when your shopping bag is small. And you don't gain economies of experience unless you're learning from everyone, so once again, you need everyone to come to the party, across a wide range of operational functions.

This tug-of-war between "above the line" (unit managers) and "below the line" (shared-service managers) is natural enough, and it might even play out as productive tension except for one thing: in most organizations, it's not a fair fight. The people leading business units tend to have more organizational clout than the people in charge of shared services. This is not to say that the business-unit leaders deserve the clout. But these managers are typically more visible. They are often sourced from the client-facing side of the business, and persuasion is what they do for a living. It doesn't help that the above-the-line team owns revenue, while the below-the-line group owns costs. In a status showdown in most organizations, revenue tends to win. FedEx is one company in which there seems to be a balance of status above and below, but it's the exception. Where is your organization on this continuum? A quick test we use is this: Who's in line to be the next CEO? What's the succession plan? If all contenders come from above the line, and there are no candidates from shared services, then the chances of a fair fight are low.

This is where strong leadership comes into play. At Yum Brands, for instance, the head of Taco Bell swore that he needed his own IT system to maintain the brand's unique advantages. Well, if Taco Bell got its own IT system, the shared-services line would be drawn too low, subtracting from the shared benefits accruing to Yum Brands. (And that's before the inevitable "If he gets his own system, why can't I?" sets in.) That's when CEO David Novak stepped in with abounding clarity, settled the dispute, and drew exactly where the line was to be. Novak is a very lovely man (let us stress lovely again), but anyone who works for him knows that it's his way or the highway on issues like these.

We will not go so far as to say that a dominant leadership style is necessary to make a shared-services model work, but empirically, where we find success, we also tend to find leaders who are willing to make powerful people in their organizations uncomfortable. And when the power brokers push back, as they often do in a reshuffling of decision rights, these leaders unapologetically hold their position. Some do it with a smile, others with a scowl, and still others with just the right amount of disinterest in the approval of others. But they all draw the line firmly. The same thing could be achieved theoretically through persuasion and consensus-building; we just haven't seen it yet. So if you find you're getting stuck in a shared-services showdown with the rainmakers in your organization, you may have to channel that internal kindergarten teacher (or drill sergeant) who is unambiguously large and in charge.

Oddly enough, one sector of the economy that has failed to draw an optimal line is a sector known for strong leadership—the military. An officer in charge of shared services once told one of us, "Our brands above the line are Army, Navy, Marine Corps, Air Force. How can that ever be a fair fight? They outrank us!" And so each branch has its own personnel system, procurement practices, and multiple customized systems for things like health care and insurance. If we look across service branches, a significant amount of potential remains unmet on both lowering costs and sharing knowledge across organizational lines.

Low Quality

The second, equally destructive obstacle to the success of shared services is when the services themselves are not world-class, and yet internal customers are forced to use them. This practice gives shared services a bad name—and reminds us of the failed conglomerates of the 1980s. This is why when some people hear "shared services," they think "forced mediocrity."

Of course, our message is the opposite. We believe that shared services are a critical part of scaling excellence, of turning one successful service model into a dynamic, growing enterprise that delivers exceptional value through multiple models. In our experience, that dream is more attainable than what the world tends to believe, but getting there requires a relationship with reality that can feel brutal at times. We wrote this chapter—and indeed, this book—to help you get more comfortable with that kind of truth.

UNCOMMON TAKEAWAYS

✓ You basically have two choices when it comes to growth: do more of what you're already doing, or do different things. In our framework, doing more of what you're already doing means growing the existing service model. Doing different things means building new service models.

✓ If you want to grow your existing service model, you must first take control of it. This typically means that you have to increase your standardization. Most organizations, it turns out, have to give up some degree of responsiveness to the needs of some customers if they want to scale the business. This doesn't have to mean, however, that you must sacrifice overall quality. You can use various strategies to defy the expected trade-off between standardized operations and the level of service a customer experiences.

✓ An alternative growth model is the multifocused firm, which means that multiple service models within the same organization are each individually optimized for a distinct operating segment, each strategically good and bad at certain things. These models often show up as distinct brands (e.g., Armani and Armani/ Exchange) or at least distinct business units. From a structural standpoint, the multifocused firm is a shared-services platform where multiple service models share at least some of the same back-office services.

✓ Multifocused firms succeed when their individual service models create some kind of mutual benefit for each other, either economies of scale or economies of experience. Organizations that achieve economies of experience are good at sharing and leveraging knowledge across service models.

✓ There are two primary barriers to making the multi-focused firm work. The first is a lack of political will to draw the line in the right place, that is, to optimally determine which services will be shared and which will stay within control of the individual service models. The second barrier is the willingness to tolerate uncompetitive quality or pricing in the company's shared services.

Conclusion

A maddening thing about service organizations is that they permit you to lie to yourself. You get to believe you can be great at everything. You get to pretend that your employees are your problem, or that your customers won't notice when your commitment to them falters. And the cost is not failure, at least not at first—just an insistent, unsatisfying mediocrity.

The antidote is honesty. The path to uncommon service goes directly, and sometimes painfully, through the mirror. Our goal in writing this book is to help you hold that mirror up to yourself and to your own organization. If you haven't averted your eyes at this point in the story, then we're optimistic about your capacity to excel.

It's of course easier for us, as outsiders, to look without blinking. But here's why we're credible in pushing you to do it. After studying the design and culture of countless organizations, we know that what you'll discover is likely to amaze you: employees who are yearning to be of service, customers who are eager to do their part, organizations that can, in fact, change overnight.

And not just organizations. In 1995, when Carlos Rodriguez-Pastor returned to Peru from the United States to take a hard look at his own family business, a financial services company known as Interbank, he saw his company's—and his country's—weaknesses with great clarity. But everywhere he looked, he also saw the potential for greatness. He saw opportunities to create unprecedented prosperity in a nation still fighting its way out of entrenched poverty and economic turmoil.

Rodriguez-Pastor bet on the future of both Interbank and Peru by building a services empire—everything from grocery stores to insurance to schools—that delivers excellence to the country's emerging middle class. The Interbank Group's $8 billion portfolio takes its inspiration from global service leaders, and its exceptional performance is fueled by an unflinching look at the gaps between its own companies and the world's best. The result? Interbank is now generating wealth for more than thirty thousand employees, who are in turn nurturing the wealth of a nation.

The way Rodriguez-Pastor tells it, the country's motto was once a dispiriting and fatalistic, "Sí, pero," which is Spanish for "Yes, but . . ." His life's ambition is to turn the country's signature phrase into "Sí, Peru." Yes, Peru. He's already made extraordinary progress. Interbank is arguably the most influential company in an economy that's now booming, at a pace that's convinced Peru's brightest minds to turn down jobs in New York and London and build their careers at home.

With the humility of someone in a much bigger game than personal advancement, Rodriguez-Pastor has a deep calm about him. His impatience for a new Peru is filtered into a careful mix of words and actions, starting with his bedrock refusal to accept mediocrity around him. He is standing for excellence, and that choice is changing a country.

People ask us all the time where they should begin. Our advice is to first believe in an alternate reality, where ordinary people create extraordinary value for customers ready to take on the world. Like Rodriguez-Pastor, you must believe in the possibility, and then look fearlessly at your distance from it.

And if you start to doubt where the journey ends, please track us down. We'd be delighted to tell you another story of uncommon service.

Introduction

1. In the case of Southwest, we're concerned about the impact of its recent merger with AirTran. It's hard to imagine how these seemingly disparate service models will integrate gracefully.

Chapter One

1. For a great discussion of Walmart's overall strategy, see David Collis and Mike Rukstad, "Can You Say What Your Strategy Is?" *Harvard Business Review,* April 2008, 82–90. This article uses the strategy maps created by Jan Rivkin. Around the world, we have seen evidence of Rivkin's pedagogy. He's a brilliant educator and generous colleague. We, and countless others, are better off for it.

2. For several more examples of challenging industry norms, see the insightful (and playful) article by Gail McGovern and Youngme Moon, "Companies and the Customers Who Hate Them," *Harvard Business Review,* June 2007, 78–84.

3. Youngme Moon, "IKEA Invades America," Case 9–0504-094 (Boston: Harvard Business School, 2004).

4. For a description of the extensive similarities between Commerce Bank and Metro Bank, see Shawn Tully, "Vernon Hill Is the Best Damn Banker Alive (Just Ask Him)," *Fortune,* September 15, 2010, http://finance.fortune.cnn.com/2010/09/15/vernon-hill-is-the-best-damn-banker-alive-just-ask-him/.

Chapter Two

1. Micheline Maynard, "At Least the Airsickness Bags Are Free," *New York Times,* August 17, 2008.

2. James L. Heskett, W. Earl Sasser Jr., and Leonard A. Schlesinger, *The Service Profit Chain* (New York: Free Press, 1997).

3. James Heskett and Earl Sasser, *Achieving Breakthrough Value* (Boston: Harvard Business School, 2003), four-CD set (no longer in distribution).

Chapter Three

1. Content on BBBK is derived from William E. Fulmer, "Bugs Burger Bug Killers, Inc. (A)," Case 9–694-018 (Used by Harvard Business School with permission of William E. Fulmer, 1990). Fulmer's sources include Tom Richman, "Getting the Bugs Out," *Inc.,* June 1984; Annette Kornblum, "Bugs Burger," *Pest Control,* November 1980; and Joan Livingston, "Absolutely Guaranteed," *Nation's Business,* November 1987. All quotations are taken from this case.

2. This is the provocatively simple concept behind Atul Gawande's best seller, *The Checklist Manifesto: How to Get Things Right* (New York: Metropolitan Books, 2010). Incorporating something as basic as a checklist into your performance management system, Gawande argues persuasively, can have dramatic effect.

3. Michael Lynn, "Restaurant Tipping and Service Quality," *Cornell Hotel and Restaurant Administration Quarterly,* February 2001.

Chapter Four

1. That is, it can't be sustained, unless you're willing to charge an enormous price premium—again, this is the Hotel Cipriani model. The data suggests that this premium must be in the neighborhood of 50 percent higher than the prices of your nearest competitor.

2. James L. Heskett, "Shouldice Hospital Limited," Case 9–683-068 (Boston: Harvard Business School, April 1983).

3. Spike Feresten, "The Soup Nazi," episode in *Seinfeld,* first aired November 2, 1995, available at www.seinfeldscripts.com/The SoupNazi.htm.

4. Dennis Campbell and Frances X. Frei, "Cost Structure, Customer Profitability, and Retention Implications of Self-Service Distribution Channels: Evidence from Customer Behavior in an Online Banking Channel," *Management Science,* January 2010.

5. http://www.zipcar.com/how/faqs/one-faq?faq_number=48.

6. http://www.zipcar.com/about/.

7. Joseph N. DiStefano, "First Union Develops Financial Heartburn," *Philadelphia Inquirer,* August 15, 1999.

8. How the company that gave birth to this innovation some-how permitted the disastrous brake failures of 2009 is a question for another book. Our short version of what happened was that the company shifted its organizing focus from improvement to growth. Relentless improvement was a worthy goal in the mind of its stake-holders (employees, partners, customers), which then manifested in rapid growth. Toyota learned that a focus on growth, however, did not necessarily manifest in improvement.

9. Scott Cook, "The Contribution Revolution: Letting Vol-unteers Build Your Business," *Harvard Business Review,* October 2008, 60–69.

10. Karim Lakhani and Zahra Kanji, "Threadless: The Busi-ness of Community," Case 9–608-707 (Boston: Harvard Business School, 2008).

Chapter Five

1. James L. Heskett, "Southwest Airlines 2002: An Industry Under Siege," Case 9–803-133 (Boston: Harvard Business School, 2003).

2. Stefan H. Thomke and Ashok Nimgade, "IDEO Product Development," Case 9–600-143 (Boston: Harvard Business School, 2007).

3. T. S. Perry, "Designing a Culture for Creativity," *Research Technology Management* 38, no. 2 (March 1995): 14–17.

4. Edgar Schein, *Organizational Culture and Leadership* (San Francisco: Jossey-Boss, 1991).

5. Charles A. O'Reilly III and Jeffrey Pfeffer, *Hidden Value: How Great Companies Achieve Extraordinary Results with Ordinary People* (Boston: Harvard Business School Press, 2000).

6. Amy Edmondson, "Psychological Safety and Learning Behavior in Work Teams," *Administrative Science Quarterly* 44, no. 4 (June 1999): 350–383.

7. Zappos, "Zappos Family Core Value #1: Deliver WOW Through Service," Zappos Web page, http://about.zappos.com/our-unique-culture/zappos-core-values/deliver-wow-through-service.

8. Zappos Staff, *Zappos 2009 Culture Book* (Las Vegas, NV: Zappos, Inc.: 2009), 28.

9. Ibid., 262.

10. Norm Brodsky, "Learning from JetBlue," *Inc.* Magazine, March 1, 2004.

11. L. Berry and K. Seltman, *Management Lessons from Mayo Clinic* (New York: McGraw-Hill, 2008), 20.

12. Ibid., 36.

Chapter Six

1. We've been energized by the exciting work that a colleague, Rob Huckman, has been doing on this topic, particularly in the area of health care.

2. We heard the story of Herb Kelleher and his response to the complaining grandmother from Earl Sasser, of Harvard Business School, in December 2006.

3. Rob Walker, "Marketing Pose," *New York Times Magazine,* July 21, 2009, www.nytimes.com/2009/07/26/magazine/26FOB-consumed-t.html?scp=1&sq=lululemon&st=cse.

4. For the best description on record of what the upstart is thinking, see Clay Christensen's classic *The Innovator's Dilemma: When New Technologies Cause Great Firms to Fail* (Boston, MA: Harvard Business School Press, 1997).

5. These stages were originally identified by psychiatrist Elizabeth Kubler-Ross as a typical pattern in confronting significant loss.

6. Material on the CDM Group is derived from interviews with Ed Wise and from Dan Maher and Dan O'Brien, "Enabling Excellence: Let Sharing Set Us Free (A and B)," Case OU-155A (2009) (internal company study at "Omnicom University," an annual executive training program of Omnicom).

Index

FRANCES FREI is the UPS Foundation Professor of Service Management at Harvard Business School and the Chair of the MBA Required Curriculum at HBS. Her research investigates how organizations can more effectively design service excellence and has been published in top-tier journals such as *Management Science* and *Harvard Business Review*. In addition, she has published dozens of case studies across a variety of industries, including financial services, government, retail, software, telecommunications, and hospitality.

Many of those case studies appear in Managing Service Operations, an elective course Frances developed to examine organizations' efforts to design, manage, and improve service experiences. She currently teaches and leads the required first-year FIELD course at HBS, which focuses on developing learning experiences that are experiential and immersive, with the overall goal of advancing the school's mission to develop leaders who make a difference in the world. She is also the Faculty Chair of the Achieving Breakthrough Service executive education program. Frances has received the HBS Student Association Faculty Award for teaching excellence on multiple occasions.

Frances regularly advises organizations seeking to create greater value through their service experiences. Her advisory work focuses on helping companies make strategic choices that allow them to profitably differentiate on service. She serves on the board of directors of Advance Auto Parts and on the boards of advisors of several private companies.

Frances received her PhD in operations and information management from the Wharton School at the University of Pennsylvania. She holds an ME in industrial engineering from Pennsylvania State University, and a BA in mathematics from the University of Pennsylvania.

Frances describes her deepest calling as helping leaders to create impact and remove "the pebbles" that can grow into obstacles to performance.

ANNE MORRISS has spent the last fifteen years working to unleash social entrepreneurs around the world. She started her career in rural Latin America, where she worked to support the development of local leaders in remote communities.

Anne is now the Managing Director of the Concire Leadership Institute, which she cofounded in 2007 to help leaders in the public, private, and nonprofit sectors to uncover and remove the barriers to excellence. She has worked with companies and governments throughout the United States and Latin America on strategy, leadership, and institutional change. Her clients have ranged from *Fortune* 50 companies repositioning in global markets to public-sector leaders working to build national competitiveness.

As a senior advisor with the OTF Group, Anne worked with the Office of President Leonel Fernandez to redesign the Dominican Republic's industrial strategy. She also advised the government of the Republic of Trinidad and Tobago on diversifying its economy away from oil and gas and developing a national entry strategy for high-tech sectors. More recently, Anne partnered with The World Bank to help leaders in forty emerging economies to increase local entrepreneurship and innovation.

Anne's career has included leading the campaign finance team for Rep. Marty Meehan and acting as the South American Director for Amigos de las Américas, an international organization that promotes community health and leadership development in Latin America. She now serves on the board of directors of GenePeeks, Inc., and chairs the board of directors of InnerCity Weightlifting, which works to promote achievement among urban youth.

Anne holds a BA in American studies from Brown University and an MBA from Harvard Business School. She has published articles in *Harvard Business Review* and *PODER Magazine*. An essay she wrote appears in *In the River They Swim: Essays from Around the World on Enterprise Solutions to Poverty.* She has lived and worked extensively in Brazil, Ecuador, Mexico, and the Dominican Republic.